Praise for

Complicit

How Greed and Collusion Made the Credit Crisis Unstoppable

by Mark Gilbert

Bloomberg News

"*Complicit* explores the devastating chain of events of 2008, offering a colorful firsthand account of instrumental players in the crisis. Mark Gilbert does an excellent job of explaining the historical relevance and current importance of events that will take years to work through, describing the policy responses and inherent risks, which will continue to impact capital markets for years to come."

—STEVEN DROBNY, Cofounder, Drobny Global Advisors
Author of *Inside the House of Money*

"Mark Gilbert brings an important and fresh examination as well as a global perspective to the recent financial crisis. *Complicit* reveals that Wall Street's bubble-inflating machinations could not have reached such destructive extremes without eager international support."

—NOMI PRINS, Senior Fellow, Demos
Author of *It Takes a Pillage*

Complicit

Also available from
Bloomberg Press

Hedge Hunters:
How Hedge Fund Masters Survived
by Katherine Burton

Confidence Game:
How a Hedge Fund Manager Called Wall Street's Bluff
by Christine Richard

———

A complete list of our titles is available at
www.bloomberg.com/books

Complicit

How Greed and Collusion Made
the Credit Crisis Unstoppable

Mark Gilbert

Bloomberg News

BLOOMBERG PRESS
NEW YORK

BLOOMBERG, BLOOMBERG ANYWHERE, BLOOMBERG.COM, BLOOMBERG MARKET ESSENTIALS, *Bloomberg Markets*, BLOOMBERG NEWS, BLOOMBERG PRESS, BLOOMBERG PROFESSIONAL, BLOOMBERG RADIO, BLOOMBERG TELEVISION, and BLOOMBERG TRADEBOOK are trademarks and service marks of Bloomberg Finance L.P. ("BFLP"), a Delaware limited partnership, or its subsidiaries. The BLOOMBERG PROFESSIONAL service (the "BPS") is owned and distributed locally by BFLP and its subsidiaries in all jurisdictions other than Argentina, Bermuda, China, India, Japan, and Korea (the "BLP Countries"). BFLP is a wholly-owned subsidiary of Bloomberg L.P. ("BLP"). BLP provides BFLP with all global marketing and operational support and service for these products and distributes the BPS either directly or through a non-BFLP subsidiary in the BLP Countries. All rights reserved.

This publication contains the author's opinions and is designed to provide accurate and authoritative information. It is sold with the understanding that the author, publisher, and Bloomberg L.P. are not engaged in rendering legal, accounting, investment-planning, or other professional advice. The reader should seek the services of a qualified professional for such advice; the author, publisher, and Bloomberg L.P. cannot be held responsible for any loss incurred as a result of specific investments or planning decisions made by the reader.

First edition published 2010
1 3 5 7 9 10 8 6 4 2

Library of Congress Cataloging-in-Publication Data

Gilbert, Mark.
    Complicit: how greed and collusion made the credit crisis unstoppable / Mark Gilbert. – 1st ed.
      p. cm.
    Includes index.
    Summary: "Reporter and editor Mark Gilbert plumbs the origins of the subprime debt crisis, tracing it back to 'a silent conspiracy of the well rewarded' in banking, real estate, trading, insurance, investing, politics, regulation, credit rating, law, and economic theory"– Provided by publisher.
    ISBN 978-1-57660-346-8 (alk. paper)
    1. Subprime mortgage loans–United States. 2. Credit–United States. 3. Financial crises–United States. 4. Mortgage banks–United States. I. Title.

HG2040.5.U5G543 2010
332.1'7530973–dc22   2009048428

Mixed Sources
Product group from well-managed forests, controlled sources and recycled wood or fibre
www.fsc.org Cert no. SW-COC-000952
© 1996 Forest Stewardship Council
FSC

CONTENTS

Introduction

The Great Credit Bubble

Where did the money come from? Where did it go? How was this allowed to happen? Who is to blame? These are the key questions surrounding the credit crunch that has engulfed the "global financial" system.

The answer, in part, is that there wasn't anywhere near as much money as there seemed to be. And because it didn't exist in the first place, the money hasn't gone anywhere. It was all an illusion, although the economic consequences of its disappearance turned out to be very real indeed.

As to how it was allowed to happen and who is to blame, in a sense the honest reply is that we all allowed it to happen, and we're all to blame, either as active accomplices or complicit bystanders. Society as a whole made a collective, unconscious decision to allow the banking system to grow unchecked because the tangible benefits that seemed to accrue from unbridled capitalism outweighed the intangible hazards that might accompany this dangerous test of capitalism's limits.

Consider an analogous bit of history. In nineteenth-century Britain, physicians finally began to understand human physiology, working out the body's geography by mapping veins and arteries, dissecting eyes and hearts, and manipulating bones and joints. The new knowledge promised to usher in a period of unprecedented medical advancement.

Religious beliefs and general distaste, however, meant that few people would send the corpses of deceased relatives to the gurneys of surgeons with eager scalpels. After all, how could a dismembered body pass through the gates of heaven? Surgeons instead dissected the bodies of executed criminals, who lost dominion over their body parts' destination upon conviction.

But—even fueled by the era's commonplace executions—supply was insufficient to meet demand. A shadowy secondary market in cadavers developed; those who died in a hospital and weren't quickly claimed by their loved ones moved from mortuaries to teaching hospitals, sold by undertakers and bought by physicians. Even those claimed by family and properly buried could be dug up and sold to satiate the needs of the anatomists.

The authorities—both legal and medical—turned a blind eye to the practice of grave robbing, while the general public remained ignorant about how doctors were getting smarter. For society as a whole, it was a win-win situation—until a pair of entrepreneurs called William Burke and William Hare decided to circumvent the waiting time demanded by nature, started murdering for profit, and brought the whole grisly, underhanded process into the open.

A similar conspiracy of vested interests caused the credit crunch. Any banker, trader, investor, or economist asked to invent the perfect financial market environment for creating global wealth beyond the wildest dreams of avarice would have come up with a list of conditions similar to those that prevailed for a decade.

Like those of Burke and Hare, these good times have ended with an almighty bang, not a whimper, wiping out the nest eggs of millions of workers by destroying stock market values around the world, undermining ordinary savers' confidence in the safety of the banking system, and exposing deep fault lines in the philosophy of capitalism. The financial community, through a deadly combination of greed and hubris, fouled its own sandpit. The era of munificent money-making conditions—regulation and oversight so gentle as to be almost invisible, ever-faster data and information flows, freely available credit at super-low interest rates, unprecedented access to investors all around the world, and oil-enriched buyers of any investment yielding north of zero—is over.

The global financial authorities—the elected politicians who decree the legal framework within which finance operates; the unelected central banks charged with tending the economy; the regulators responsible for creating and enforcing safety rules; the money managers entrusted with nurturing the future incomes of widows, orphans, and hordes of other savers; and the people paying themselves millions of dollars to run the investment banks—all looked the other way. They operated under the belief that the monetary benefits accruing to society from incessant, unprecedented, and essentially unregulated growth in the securities industry more than outweighed any of the attendant risks.

In the United States the rising economic tide was seen to lift all boats, underlining the political triumph of capitalism over socialism and communism. In Europe, increased prosperity helped cement the decades-old dream of a common currency, binding nations closely enough to nullify the nagging conflicts that gave rise to two world wars, with the United Kingdom playing a supporting role as the un-official treasurer to its continental, euro-embracing neighbors, even as it clung stubbornly to its own currency. And across swathes of Asia, globalization and growing international trade helped fund the transition from agrarian to manufacturing economies, with governments offering compensatory affluence to avert discussions about democracy and voting systems, thereby blunting the risk of social unrest.

The list of credit crunch perpetrators is long. Realtors appraised houses at fictitious levels. Lenders granted mortgages to people who couldn't pay. Aspiring homeowners bought properties that they couldn't afford, taking on debt burdens they couldn't support. Frankenstein bankers cobbled together nasty parts of different markets, creating instruments they couldn't value or control. Credit-rating companies stamped their highest seals of approval on nearly anything and everything that crossed their desks. Traders invented prices they couldn't justify. Investors bought securities they didn't understand. And there are thousands and thousands of fleas on the financial dog; armies of lawyers and accountants earned their livings during the past decade by pretending to scrutinize deals while getting paid for rubber-stamping transactions.

The people in the world of high finance aren't stupid. For at least a decade, the finest graduates of universities all over the globe have been drawn to Wall Street and its counterparts in the world's biggest cities. Little wonder, then, that market regulators struggled to either find or retain talented staff, when the rewards for jumping the fence and becoming a poacher rather than a gamekeeper were so rich. Investment banks and hedge funds became employment black holes, sucking in talent to the detriment of arguably more productive, clearly less lucrative, disciplines such as engineering and science.

The credit crunch wasn't caused so much by a confederacy of dunces as by a silent conspiracy of the well rewarded. And most of the participants aren't fraudsters (albeit with some notable exceptions), nor are they evil or malicious. But everyone involved collectively suspended disbelief, a mass self-induced myopia to the possibility that anything could go wrong, because the financial rewards for playing along were so compelling.

One of the simplest tricks in finance involves borrowing money at a low rate of interest, reinvesting it at a higher rate, and pocketing the difference. The easiest way to achieve this is to take out a short-term loan which, because it will be repaid quickly, typically offers a low interest rate. Then invest the proceeds in some longer-term investment, which offers a higher payout because it locks away the money for a longer period.

When the initial loan falls due, the investor simply takes out a second loan to repay the first, then a third loan to repay the second, and so on until the longer-term investment project pays off and all debts are covered, plus a nice profit. Banks have always done this, taking in deposits from customers who get a low interest rate and instant access to their money, then lending that cash at higher rates to governments building tarmac roads and erecting bridges, and to companies building factories and buying equipment. The difference between rates is called the spread, and it's a fundamental bank profit driver.

The credit crunch revealed that the financial community had made similar spread bets billions of times over, relying on short-term loans to make wildly speculative purchases of an array of increasingly complicated derivatives securities. The system didn't have an alternative source of financing when short-term loans started to dry up amid concerns about liquidity and solvency, leaving investors with no way to cover their bets when derivative market investments lost value.

Since its inception, the derivatives market has echoed the fairground hawker's call to "scream if you want to go faster." Every time Microsoft Corporation upgrades its Excel spreadsheet software to accommodate more cells, rows, and columns, the structured finance world grafts yet more layers of complexity onto its inventions. Once investment banks found ways to decouple derivatives from underlying markets, constraints on how much product they could create and how big the bets could become disappeared, creating a new universe of virtual money.

Regulation failed to keep pace with those changes. None of the global economy's health and safety inspectors showed up for work during the past decade. No one wanted to be responsible for slowing the output of the financial factory with pesky citations for violating the rules, let alone threaten parts of it with closure.

Central banks said it wasn't their role to second guess when a bubble might be swelling and not their place to do anything except clean up the mess a puncture might cause. Regulators left some areas, such as the over-the-counter derivatives that aren't listed on any exchange, to their own devices. Others became the province of credit-rating companies, which made money in defiance of the inherent conflict of interest.

All these market overseers convinced themselves that credit derivatives were a neat way to slice and dice markets into separate components with greater or lesser chances of losing money, which could then be distributed more evenly and safely through the financial system to those with the appropriate risk appetite. Market overseers, though, missed the trick: the derivatives desks at major banks invented bets that had never existed before, creating risk out of thin air rather than simply refining and redistributing existing exposures.

While the current crisis is unprecedented in its scale, it is untrue to say that nobody saw it coming. Plenty of market commentators screamed from the rooftops about the trouble ahead, warning that the clothing worn by the emperors of finance was threadbare at best and likely to unravel in a storm. Shouting that the king was in the nude was a thankless and futile exercise, though, while market liquidity was flowing freely; as billionaire investor Warren Buffett said, it is only when the tide goes out that the world learns who has been swimming naked. None of the participants had any incentive to check whether their Speedos were slipping during the boom times.

Capitalism will always overreach itself, which goes a long way toward explaining why it is such a successful economic motivator. It rewards those who put their reputations and money on the line. Typically, the bigger the gamble, the bigger the potential gain. But even laissez-faire capitalism should punish mistakes, and that essential constraint disappeared during the go-go years.

It is almost impossible for the average person to comprehend just how much money finance professionals paid themselves during the boom times. In the investment banking world, a base salary of $100,000 is walking-around money, the loose change used to pay for incidentals. The real prize comes in the bonus. While mere mortals focus on the left-hand side of their pay slips, hoping to turn $35,000 into $37,000 or $64,000 into $69,000, the masters of the financial universe are much more interested in the right-hand side of the number, trying to add the zeroes that augment $100,000 with a bonus of $1,000,000 or $10,000,000.

No wonder investment bank brass spent zero time trying to understand how their employees were actually generating quarterly profit numbers. Asking questions about what kinds of risks employees were running might have produced unwelcome answers, imperiling those lovely bonus payments.

U.S. President Barack Obama was spot on when he called those payments "the height of irresponsibility. It is shameful." In his subsequent request, though, for "the folks on Wall Street who are asking for help to show some restraint and show some discipline and show some sense of responsibility," he may as well have been speaking in tongues. Restraint, discipline, and responsibility have not been part of the financial world's lexicon for years.

A January 2009 report by the New York State comptroller estimated that, even in the eye of the credit-crunch hurricane in 2008, Wall Street firms paid themselves $18.4 billion in bonuses while passing their begging bowls among U.S. taxpayers. John Thain, in his final year as head of Merrill Lynch before Bank of America bought that firm and jettisoned Thain, signed off on a $1.2 million office refurbishment package that included $87,000 for rugs and more than $35,000 for a commode on legs. (Thain ultimately agreed to repay costs out of his own pocket.)

The bankers alone aren't to blame, of course, any more than the grave robbers of the nineteenth century were solely responsible for the medical profession's sourcing strategies. As a whole, the financial community "behaved as if untethered by any moral or social account-ability," according to Tim Price, the investment director at PFP Wealth

Management in London. "Just when capitalism seemed to have won the global battle for consumer hearts and minds, its venal banking sector had sown the seeds for its own destruction and replacement by a newly resurgent spirit of socialism and protectionism."

In the latter part of the twentieth century, it was Milton Friedman, rather than John Maynard Keynes, who shaped the economic policies of Western governments. The twenty-first century will show that, while capitalism triumphed in the battle against socialism, it may not have won the war.

ONE

Bubbles Are for Bathtubs

The Real Estate Boom

Everything's inflated, like a tire on a car. Well, the man came and took my Chevy back, I'm glad I hid my old guitar.
— BOB DYLAN, "MONEY BLUES"

IN 2005, JAMIE WESTENHISER, Playboy Enterprises' Playmate of the Month for May of that year, announced that her disrobing days were over. With housing prices near her home in Fort Lauderdale, Florida, up 105 percent in the previous five years, the then-23-year-old model told the magazine she was quitting the skin game for a career in real estate. The Playboy Bunny swapped a profession specializing in artificially inflated assets for a career focused on, well, artificially inflated assets. Westenhiser made her move just as U.S. housing reached its least affordable level in the five years since the National Association of Realtors began tracking median home prices against incomes.

The seeds of the global credit crunch were sowed in the housing market. It was fertile ground, nourished by a booming economy and

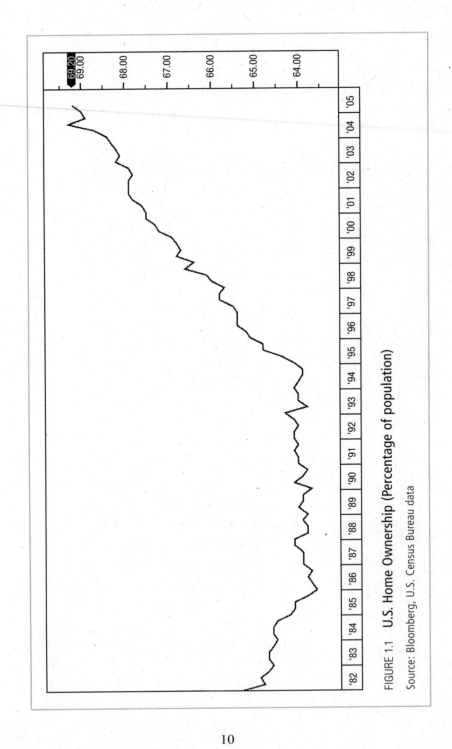

FIGURE 1.1 **U.S. Home Ownership (Percentage of population)**

Source: Bloomberg, U.S. Census Bureau data

10

watered by a misguided belief that the good times would never end and housing prices would never fall. All of the credit crunch villains played a role in inflating the real estate bubble, including ordinary people borrowing beyond their means to buy their dream properties or simply gamble for profit, market regulators averting their eyes from the growing pile of unsafe mortgages, and investment bankers who were able to weave ordinary home loans into complex financial products to be bought and sold all around the world.

Suspending Disbelief

Houses and apartments, typically slow to build, sometimes hard to sell, and easily the most expensive purchases most people ever make, were once considered a long-term commitment. Buyers needed verifiable incomes and good credit scores to get mortgages. In this market, however, it became akin to sacrilege to admit that some consumers couldn't handle a mortgage. Banks loved the possibility of writing and packaging more mortgages—and earning the attendant fees. Investors were eager to buy those mortgages. Politicians loved the idea of poorer constituents getting a foothold in the housing market, making for more stable communities—and potentially more winnable votes.

The housing market became a Ponzi scheme, where the cash from the new entrants was passed up the pyramid to give the illusion of rising profits. That worked when prices were rising, but proved disastrous when values started to subside, a slide that triggered the credit crunch. Banks lent money against a backdrop of rising housing values, so people felt as if they were better off. In truth, though, the churning market created little real wealth. The foundations of the housing boom crumbled easily because they were made of borrowed money.

To maintain the charade, the market needed a strong supply of new prospective homeowners—ideally, ones who would suspend any disbelief in forever-increasing home values. In the 1980s, about 64 percent of Americans owned their own homes, according to figures collected by the U.S. Census Bureau. As mortgages became more freely available, that percentage jumped to about 69 percent by the middle of 2004—a large jump, given how stable homeownership figures had been for decades, and one that probably incorporated the most marginally qualified buyers. It stuck there for the following three years, then slipped to 68 percent in 2007 and 2008 as the housing market collapsed.

Many of those latecomers would never have qualified for a mortgage under normal circumstances. But because the people at every link in the housing chain had a stake in keeping the music playing for as long as possible, the hindmost were welcomed into the homeowning fold, where membership qualifications grew more and more lax. These changing credit standards formed the "credit" side of the credit crunch.

Bubbles Are for Bathtubs

The financial bubble that grew up around the U.S. housing market also needed experienced buyers to suspend their powers of reason and adopt the belief that housing prices would continue ever upward. "Bubbles are for bathtubs," was the marketing message at http://www.condoflip.com, a Web site exhorting Americans to jump on the get-rich bandwagon by "flipping" properties. Some bought and sold existing homes; others went so far as buying developer-planned condominiums, then selling them to the next speculator, at a profit, before construction crews even broke ground.

Poor stock market returns also stoked increased appetite for American real estate. The Nasdaq Composite Index lost almost half its value from March to December of 2000. A wave of accounting scandals followed that slump, engulfing companies such as Enron

Corporation and WorldCom, and undermining investor confidence in the veracity of company earnings. From a peak of 5,132 points in March 2000, the Nasdaq index tumbled more than 70 percent in the next three years.

Many investors were disappointed by the stock market; to them, real estate looked like a better place to invest a nest egg. That helped explain why U.S. housing prices were climbing at an annual pace of 12.5 percent by the first quarter of 2005, according to the Office of Federal Housing Enterprise Oversight. The housing market had already seen an annualized gain of 11.9 percent in the previous three months and 13.4 percent in the third quarter of 2004.

For the housing pyramid to stay upright, every new owner had to believe that housing prices would continue to rise indefinitely. But the global housing market's history shows very clearly that housing bubbles don't deflate—they burst. There is plenty of evidence, too, to suggest that bursting real estate values can often wreak economic chaos.

Thomas Helbling, deputy chief of the world economic studies division at the International Monetary Fund in Washington, DC, scrutinized the housing market histories of fourteen industrialized nations for the period from 1970 to 2002, finding seventy-five home-price cycles. Bull housing markets typically lasted a bit less than three years, he found, with prices climbing by a cumulative, inflation-adjusted 11 percent. Bear housing markets were about one year long and decreased prices by about 6 percent, his study found.

In more extreme times, which Helbling felt defined 25 percent of the cycles, boom times lasted for about four years and brought an average increase in housing values of 32 percent. Housing market busts also persisted for about four years, with prices declining by an average of 27 percent. Helbling presented his findings at the IMF's October 2003 conference on Real Estate Indicators and Financial Stability.

There was no question that what was happening in the U.S. counted as an extreme boom, according to Helbling's measurements.

The average price of a U.S. single-family home more than doubled between the beginning of 1989 and June 2003, climbing to $229,000 from $113,000, according to figures compiled by the National Association of Realtors. Housing prices then gained an additional 20 percent, peaking at an average of $278,000 by June 2007. According to Helbling's analysis, real estate professionals should by then have been braced for a four-year bust, one that would erase housing values by about a quarter.

The housing market, moreover, was deeply integrated with the wider economy, and historical evidence shows the power of slumping property values to wreck the economy. "Housing price busts in industrial countries were associated with substantial negative output gaps, as real gross domestic product growth decreases noticeably," Helbling wrote in his study. "On average, the output level three years after the beginning of a housing price bust was about 8 percent below the level that would have prevailed with the average growth rate during the three years up to the bust." In other words, allowing housing prices to climb unchecked is a risky route to a prosperity that typically proves short-lived and results in a ferocious hangover.

Some commentators began to get nervous about how the most recent bubble's endgame might look. In 2005, Yale University economist Robert J. Shiller updated his prescient 2000 stock market book *Irrational Exuberance*, adding a new section on the housing market. He told the *New York Times* in August of that year that U.S. housing prices might decline by as much as 40 percent in the next generation. Shiller dug into price data back to the late 1800s to conclude that a period of declining prices followed every boom.

David Rosenberg, then chief economist for North America at Merrill Lynch in New York, concluded in an August 2005 research report that U.S. houses for first-time buyers were at their least affordable since the third quarter of 1989, when rising energy prices and higher Federal Reserve interest rates had last coincided with a bursting bubble. History, moreover, taught a hard lesson about what might come next. In his report he wrote that, in 1989, "new home sales plunged 20 percent in the ensuing year as demand responded to the affordability erosion."

But these comments had little effect on central bank attitudes toward asset bubbles. Central bank philosophy remained strictly agnostic. Policy makers would deal with the aftershocks, if any, caused by bursting bubbles, but they would not target asset prices. They hadn't tried to talk investors out of driving equity prices to untenable levels earlier in the decade, after all; Federal Reserve then-chairman Alan Greenspan declined to repeat his December 1996 comment that "irrational exuberance" (the origin of Shiller's book title) might be a shaky foundation on which to build such gains.

Central bankers were not about to risk a backlash by trying to restrain real estate values, and so the most recent boom drew few official warnings. The nearest was a milquetoast comment from Greenspan in July 2005, who said he saw "signs of froth in some local markets." Housing prices continued to rise unchecked.

Houses as ATMs

Rising prices let consumers use their homes as gigantic cash machines, buying Chevrolet behemoths, wall-dominating high-definition plasma television screens, and every shiny toy Apple waved under their gadget-guzzling snouts. Savings accounts became as unfashionable as mullet haircuts as homeowners piled on debt, assuming that real estate prices would keep rising, allowing home equity to support the lifestyles to which they were quickly growing accustomed.

U.S. homeowners extracted a record $223 billion from rising real estate values in the second quarter of 2005, up from $134 billion in the year-earlier period and from just $77 billion in the second three months of 2000, according to estimates of net equity release compiled by the Federal Reserve. Almost 75 percent of the mortgage refinancing in April, May, and June of 2005 was driven by homeowners looking for extra cash, not better mortgage terms, according to the U.S. government-sponsored mortgage company Freddie Mac.

Ninja Loans

A brand of financial engineering known as securitization served as the crucial catalyst for new and refinanced mortgages. Mortgage companies were able to lend homebuyers money, then sell those mortgages to a third party—a big improvement over waiting 25 or 30 years for repayment, as banks do if they hold a mortgage. The third party, meanwhile, could buy loans from multiple mortgage companies, bundle them together, and sell them to investors, using monthly mortgage payments to fund regular interest payments to purchasers. The first bank then earned fees from originating and administrating the mortgage. This process was the kindling that made the credit crunch so incendiary.

Because mortgage companies could sell the loans they originated for cash, they stopped caring about what might happen to those loans in the future. They began to prioritize volume over quality, offering low teaser rates in the secure knowledge that eventual increases—and borrowers' ability to pay them—would be someone else's problem. The shift dismantled the historical relationship between lenders and borrowers, prompting the relaxation and then abandonment of mortgage lending standards.

No immediate, unsavory consequences resulted from imprudent lending, giving banks no incentive to guard against unwise policies. Reckless lenders earned more fee income than their competitors, making their businesses grow faster. Prudent lenders suffered in comparison and, in a rational response, followed their competitors in abandoning good practices.

Loans needing little or no proof of income from the borrower increased to $276 billion, or 46 percent, of all subprime mortgages granted in 2006, up from just $30 billion in 2001, according to estimates made in 2007 by New York–based analysts at Credit Suisse Group. A 2006 study cited by the Mortgage Asset Research Institute showed that almost 60 percent of borrowers whose incomes weren't checked overstated their earnings by at least 50 percent. No wonder they became known as "liar loans" or, more poetically, "Ninja loans," to describe borrowers who had No Income, No Job or Assets. So-called negative amortization mortgages, where the monthly payments aren't even enough to cover the interest on the loan and the accruing deficit is continuously added to the amount outstanding, are a particularly egregious example of how far some lenders were willing to bend over backwards to prevent an inability to pay from deterring potential customers.

Financial authorities did little to rein in housing prices or remind banks of basic lending standards, even as the bubble grew. Some market predictors did see the possibility of a collapse in U.S. housing prices. Merrill's Rosenberg warned in August 2005 that he was "convinced that the housing market is ripe for a price correction." As he predicted, "Bubbles usually end, not necessarily because of higher interest rates, but because you eventually reach a price point where the bids dry up. When you treat your rising home price as a bonus to be spent every year, and that source of so-called income dries up, so does your economic activity." No one, however, who was in a position to puncture the housing bubble had anything to gain from seeing prices falter.

Central bankers, whose responsibility it was to snatch away the punchbowl whenever a party threatened to get too wild, had no interest in restraining the housing market. Higher housing prices helped restrain wage growth. Unearned capital increases on real estate replaced pay demands as the route many people took to participate in the booming U.S. and European economies. And while central banks professed a lack of faith in their ability to identify or deal with bubbles, they were united in their belief that higher wages would unleash inflation. So the U.S. Federal Reserve, the European Central Bank, and the Bank of England occasionally commented on the risks of financial inebriation. Mostly, though, they just congratulated each other on hosting a swell economic party.

The Federal Reserve Board also contributed to the housing boom by keeping the cost of money too cheap for too long. Its official target rate, which sets the pace for consumer lending costs, was 6 percent at the beginning of 2001. By the end of that year, the U.S. central bank had slashed its policy rate to 1.75 percent, with further reductions driving it to 1 percent in the middle of 2003. In the decade preceding 2002, the Fed target rate had averaged 4.8 percent. From the beginning of 2002 until the end of 2004, however, it averaged just 1.4 percent, helping to fuel a borrowing binge.

And when the central bank did begin raising rates in the middle of 2004, mortgage lenders didn't curtail their lending. Instead, they loosened their borrowing standards to maintain the deal flow.

Toxic Loans

By then, the housing market was out of control and beginning to unravel. Problem loans, originated by lenders and passed on to investors through the securitization process, were starting to bear their toxic fruit, as borrowers defaulted or missed payments.

Mortgage companies were the first hit hard by the burgeoning crisis. The rapid demise of New Century Financial Corporation, based in Irvine, California, showed how unsafe the subprime mortgage business was, and how lenders depended on the oxygen of bank loans to stay alive.

New Century, which was founded in 1995, granted home loans worth $220 billion, becoming the second-biggest player in the subprime lending market. In February 2007, New Century told the authorities it was restating its financial results for the previous year, provoking the U.S. Justice Department to begin a criminal investigation of

New Century executives. In the following weeks, regulators in states including New York, New Jersey, and Massachusetts accused New Century of failing to deliver funds it had pledged to new customers.

New Century, of course, didn't have the money to fulfill its promises. It had relied on selling its mortgages to investment banks and borrowing from its bank credit lines. As more and more of its existing subprime borrowers got into payment difficulties, investors were less interested in buying the mortgages, and bankers were unwilling to issue new loans. Together, they turned off the taps and shut New Century down.

The most astonishing aspect of New Century's failing business model, revealed as part of its April 2007 bankruptcy petition, is how ferociously it treaded water in its final months, making a desperate effort to stay afloat. New Century granted loans worth $60 billion in 2006 alone—more than a quarter of all the business it ever undertook during its twelve-year lifespan—as it pumped out more and more loans it hoped to sell for repackaging, trying to keep the credit flowing.

Subprime lenders, who typically made loans to borrowers with sketchy credit, weren't the only part of the mortgage market spinning out of control. A company called American Home Mortgage Investment Corporation specialized in alternative A mortgages. Alt-A, as it was called, was a catch-all classification for loans made to borrowers, such as self-employed workers, who didn't meet the standards for "prime" classification, but didn't score low enough to drop into the "subprime" category.

American Home Mortgage also relied on bank loans to stay in business. As the subprime infection spread and alt-A borrowers began missing mortgage payments, the company tried to buy time by telling its customers, in May 2007, that they could make monthly home loan payments using American Express credit cards. Three months later, American Home Mortgage also filed for bankruptcy protection.

Being in the mortgage business was like riding a bicycle: keep the wheels turning or fall off. New Century and American Home Mortgage were typical of the new breed of housing financiers. They focused on originating loans and then selling them, using the cash to finance more business. When those loans started to sour, the mortgage companies crashed to the ground. By the middle of 2007, more than fifty subprime lenders had either gone bust or tried to sell themselves to peers and rivals.

Mortgage companies weren't the only ones threatened by the decaying housing market. Those toxic mortgages had spread far and wide throughout the global financial system. About a month after New Century disintegrated, the holes in the subprime mortgage market captured a banking victim. UBS AG, which was then the world's biggest manager of other people's money, announced in May 2007 that it was winding down its Dillon Read Capital Management LLC hedge fund unit after wrong-way bets on the mortgage market cost it about 150 million Swiss francs. "The area that gave us some trouble was the subprime space," said John Costas, who had run the fund since June 2005 for UBS after four years as head of the bank's securities unit.

The subprime contagion was metastasizing. It had moved from buyers using adjustable rate mortgages to purchase overpriced houses, to the brokers who provided subprime and alt-A mortgages, then moved on to investment bankers who packed multiple mortgages into virtual boxes, forming investments called credit derivatives. They persuaded Moody's Investors Service and Standard & Poor's to give the boxes AAA credit ratings, then sold those boxes to investors who didn't care what their box contained, so long as the monthly statements looked healthy and returns to investors continued to rise.

When mortgage rates adjusted, homebuyers realized that they couldn't afford their new payments. Worse, the value of their homes had dropped too far to allow them to negotiate new loans. They stopped making payments. Investors, no longer certain of getting their money back, began to care very much what their boxes contained. By then however, it was too late. Companies that had invested in subprime mortgage–backed securities saw earnings and share prices drop, and heads began to roll.

A Crunch Heard 'Round the World

Even during its inception, the credit boom that became a crunch was a global phenomenon. It wasn't just American mortgages that were repackaged and sold around the world, nor was the United States the only nation caught in the grip of a mania for bricks and mortar. If anything, Americans were a bit behind the times, given what had happened elsewhere, and could have learned valuable lessons from the riches-to-rags experiences of other nations.

In Australia, for example, 2000 saw an 8.3 percent average annual increase in housing prices. A year later, that pace accelerated to more than 11 percent. In 2002 and 2003, Australians could count on their homes becoming at least 17 percent more valuable every quarter. The Australian central bank responded by raising interest rates, pushing its key overnight rate half a point higher to 4.75 percent in 2002, to 5.25 percent by the end of 2003, and to 5.5 percent in early 2005, a tacit recognition that policy had been too lax for too long.

As those higher borrowing costs drove up mortgage payments, Australia's housing market rapidly cooled. Prices grew 12.6 percent in the second quarter of 2004, 8.2 percent in the third, and 2.7 percent in the final three months of the year. In the first quarter of 2005, they rose just 0.4 percent. The lesson was clear: housing prices did not have to climb inexorably.

The U.K. housing market provided the scariest horror story, illustrating one among the many bad things that can happen when a supercharged housing market comes off the rails. The average price of a London property almost doubled in the four years before the second quarter of 1989, climbing to £97,667, according to figures compiled by the mortgage lender Nationwide Building Society. Londoners who bought property in mid-1979 nearly quadrupled their money in ten years, twice the return they could have gotten from U.K. stocks.

Across the United Kingdom housing prices enjoyed a similar though less dramatic surge, with the average value climbing to a bit more than £62,000 by the middle of 1989, up from £34,700 four years earlier and £19,075 in 1979. If bragging about home values at dinner parties had been an Olympic sport, Britons would have topped the medal tally.

As in the United States poor stock market returns helped fuel rising home prices. A stock market collapse in 1987 had helped inflate property prices. In October and November of that year, the Financial Times–Stock Exchange 100 Index of leading U.K. stocks plummeted, losing more than a third of its value in less than five weeks. British property started to look like a much safer place than the equity market to squirrel away retirement cash.

The downturn, when it arrived, was devastating. By the end of 1992, the average London property was worth less than £67,000, according to Nationwide's figures, a drop of more than a third. Nationally, property prices slumped by about 24 percent from the middle of 1989 to the end of 1992, leaving many people underwater, owing more to their mortgage lenders than their houses were worth.

Surging interest rates and rising unemployment fueled price slumps. The United Kingdom doubled its benchmark lending rate to 15 percent in October 1989, from as low as 7.5 percent in May 1988. Even by the middle of 1992, the official policy rate was still as high as 10 percent. From 1986 to 1990, the U.K. unemployment rate had halved, reaching as low as 5.2 percent in April 1990. It took less than two years to climb back near double figures, reaching 9.9 percent by December 1992.

Ripple effects took a severe toll on the broader economy. U.K. monthly retail sales enjoyed average annual growth of 6.4 percent in 1988. Sales growth slumped to an average 2 percent in 1989. In 1991, purchases declined in every month except November, posting an average fall of 1.4 percent. Retailers eked out a rally of just 0.8 percent in 1992.

Bonfire Kindling

All around the world, then, housing booms generated unprecedented demand for new loans. Lax oversight meant borrowers could have poorer credit and less proof of earnings than in the past. Securitization gave lenders a way to swiftly earn fees, sell loans, and move on to the next borrower. And central banks basked in the glow of a hot, vibrant economy without any sign that inflation might spoil the good times. Just as shoeshine boys who offered stock tips telegraphed the equity market peak before the Great Crash of 1929, a stripper signaled the top of the U.S. housing market in the middle of this decade by ditching photo shoots for real estate.

Wall Street had a growing pile of mortgages to use as kindling. It was time to build a financial bonfire.

TWO

Unsafe at Any Rating

CDOs and the Companies That Judged Them

*The range of derivatives contracts is limited only by the imagination
of man or sometimes, so it seems, madmen.*

—BILLIONAIRE INVESTOR WARREN BUFFETT
IN THE 2003 EDITION OF HIS ANNUAL LETTER TO
SHAREHOLDERS OF BERKSHIRE HATHAWAY

IT IS NO COINCIDENCE THAT IN 2006, *at the same time that the U.S.
housing market rocketed, the global derivatives market grew at the
fastest pace on record. The total amount outstanding climbed by an
unprecedented 40 percent to an incredible $415 trillion, according
to figures compiled by the Bank for International Settlements.*

Derivatives created the conduit through which a flood of unsafe
mortgages—created in the promiscuous housing boom—flowed out
into every nook and cranny of the investment universe, like time-
release poisons. The market for derivative securities boomed as
investors, including typically conservative buyers such as pension
funds, threw caution to the wind and purchased ever-more complex

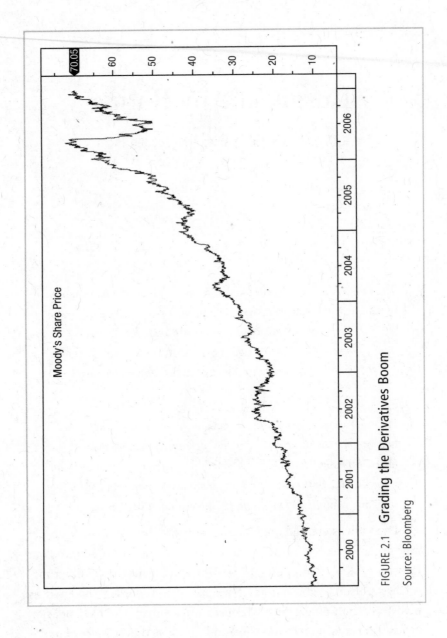

Moody's Share Price

FIGURE 2.1   Grading the Derivatives Boom

Source: Bloomberg

26

structures. The promise of benchmark-beating returns, they hoped, would head off the threat that hedge funds would steal clients by offering better profits.

Almost all the explosive derivatives growth was in investments called over-the-counter securities, to distinguish them from products listed on and regulated by exchanges. Investment banks resisted any effort to introduce common templates and shift the growing derivatives business onto the exchanges because they could charge more for tailor-made, individual contracts. Private deals also attracted less scrutiny than exchange-traded products, with their higher public visibility. If sunlight is the best antiseptic, derivatives were more akin to mushrooms, grown most profitably in the dark.

Among the new derivatives, collateralized-debt obligations (CDOs) were particularly hot. To make a CDO, bankers bundle together a package of other kinds of securities, such as corporate bonds, asset-backed securities (ABSs), or credit-default swaps (CDSs), that are tied to company creditworthiness or mortgage performance. By carving the resulting collections into slices of differing quality, the creators can make the riskiest portions absorb any losses on the underlying assets first, thereby cushioning the higher-rated slices.

As with nearly every other investment vehicle, CDOs were designed to reward investors according to the amount of risk they took. Those who bought lower-risk securities typically earned a smaller rate of return from successful investments than did those who took bigger risks, who received either a larger payoff if the investment performed well, or nothing at all if the investment failed. Trouble was, no one had a clear idea of just how risky any given slice was, or any sense of how to quantify and value that risk.

In the same way that Liverpudlians disguise overripe meat and vegetables by cooking them to mush in a stew called scouse, investment banks, ratings companies, and plain old market peer pressure turned the investments inside most CDOs from inedible chunks of the financial markets into bite-size morsels palatable to pension fund trustees. No pension fund—and only a few other investors—would buy a structured transaction whose worth depends on what happens to the stock market and company creditworthiness, which way commodity prices go, and whether the wind blows on a Sunday. They did, however, happily purchase CDOs that offered strong credit ratings and the promise of top-flight returns.

CDOs also allowed fund managers to circumvent investment rules as they chased higher yields. In September 2004, for example, Caisse des Depots et Consignations, which was then France's biggest financial institution, created a four-part CDO worth €70 million. Though the CDO was marketed as a debt instrument, purchasers in essence made a complicated bet on the creditworthiness and stock prices of a basket of companies. Fund managers who were only allowed to buy bonds could use CDOs to make stock market bets without breaching fund rules.

Wall Street was finding ways to corral just about every kind of financial gamble into bond-like products, which found a much wider audience than would highly speculative investments sold directly, as stand-alone bets. Investors who would never have lent money to homebuyers with poor credit ended up owning bad mortgages.

CDO buyers didn't know how many CDOs depended on subprime mortgages because they paid no attention to examining the ingredients that had been boiled together to brew the CDOs they acquired. Instead, they relied on a series of assessments known as credit ratings, designed to give an at-a-glance picture of a security's relative risk. The best-rated securities are considered most likely to repay lenders; the worst typically offer the possibility of higher yields, but are less likely to repay investors.

Collusion and Conflict

Three companies dominate the credit-rating business: Moody's Investors Service, Standard and Poor's, and Fitch Ratings. Provided one of these three ratings companies described an investment as worthy of an AAA grade, the highest possible, most CDO investors could close their eyes and buy. They didn't even have to understand how ratings companies had reached their conclusions, or worry whether the mathematical models used truly incorporated all possible risk.

Buying a top-rated CDO was, in theory, as safe as lending to the U.S. government by buying Treasury bonds. In theory. "For investors, a triple A rating became the stamp of approval that said this investment is safe," said Henry Waxman, chairman of the U.S. House of Representatives Committee on Oversight and Government Reform, in his opening statement for the October 2008 hearing, Credit Rating Agencies and the Financial Crisis. "And for Wall Street's investment banks, a triple A rating became the independent validation that turned a pool of risky home loans into a financial goldmine."

By relying on ratings, both buyers and sellers relinquished responsibility for doing any due diligence on what was bought and sold in the credit boom. At the time, due diligence wasn't a high priority for anyone in the food chain that produced and consumed CDOs. The banks, which wanted to make the new specials on the menu as toothsome as possible, paid ratings companies for their services. You wouldn't trust a restaurant that paid for its Zagat Survey rating. Investors, however, didn't view CDO ratings with similar distaste. Credit ratings allowed them to buy investments— and pursue potential returns—that would have otherwise been forbidden to them, either by rules that allowed a fund to buy only bonds, or by the strictures of a typical investment fund, which disallow the purchase of unrated securities no matter how juicy the promised returns.

Buyer, seller, and middleman all benefited when a CDO secured a rating. Sellers found a ready market for even their most esoteric products, buyers could offer their clients turbocharged returns, and the credit-rating companies received a fee for blessing the transactions.

The conflict of interest was obvious. Gretchen Morgenson, writing for the *New York Times* in December 2008, summarized the issue with a quote from a Moody's vice president, published in the *Christian Science Monitor* in 1957. "We obviously cannot ask payment for rating a bond," Edmund Vogelius told the newspaper half a century ago. "To do so would attach a price to the process and we could not escape the charge, which would undoubtedly come, that our ratings are for sale."

The higher the grade an investment receives, the wider the potential buying audience, because some funds have rules that insist on investments of a particular quality. If a CDO's sellers didn't like the initial verdict from one ratings company, they could threaten to take their business next door. Ongoing conversations between seller and endorser ensured that a CDO got the tweaks necessary for a desirable bond rating—and ensured that everyone involved in the process got paid. There was a frightening amount of collusion involved in assembling a CDO and getting it to market with an investor-impressing, sale-ensuring seal of approval.

Ratings companies' importance surged as regulators sought to enshrine credit ratings in accounting and investment rules. The authority of ratings became unquestionable, provided that no one questioned their veracity. Moody's, S&P, and Fitch appeared to be independent, impartial arbiters of creditworthiness, when they were really nothing of the sort.

"People view them as important and act on the basis of that understanding—even if it proves impossible for analysts to actually isolate the specific benefits the agencies generate for these market actors," writes Timothy J. Sinclair, who teaches international political economy at the University of Warwick in England, in *The New Masters of Capital: American Bond Rating Agencies and the Politics of Creditworthiness*, published by Cornell University Press in 2005. "What is central to the status and consequentiality of rating agencies is what people believe about them and act on collectively, even if those beliefs are demonstrably false."

In his book, Sinclair argues that the ratings companies began to supplant banks as the "gatekeepers" of capital. Previously, banks stood in the middle by accepting deposits and lending that money to borrowers. Both borrower and lender had a contractual relationship with the bank, rather than with each other. The growth of the securities markets diluted that relationship, in a process called disintermediation. "Judgments about who receives credit and who does not are no longer centralized in banks, as was the case in the past," Sinclair writes. "Over the past decade, the liberalization of financial markets has made rating increasingly important as a form of private regulation."

Market participants increasingly viewed credit ratings as discoverable, objective, universal truths, rather than subjective assessments based on incomplete information about what the future might hold. The feedback loop between CDO sellers and assayers, with everyone employing and even sharing the same mathematical assumptions and spreadsheet models, left no room for dissent—but lots of opportunity for participants to conspire.

Not-So-Crystal Balls

For the game to work, everyone involved had to turn a blind eye to the less-than-stellar track record assembled by the ratings companies that assessed CDOs. And they did—until CDOs' poor performance became impossible to ignore. Of the CDOs that started with AAA ratings in January 2002, 16 percent had lost that top grade by November 2004. Almost 14 percent of second-tier AA-rated securities were cut, and nearly 17 percent of CDOs with third-level, A-category ratings suffered a downgrade.

Those early CDOs, which typically contained vanilla corporate bonds, were hurt by a swift deterioration in average creditworthiness, combined with some hefty one-off defaults, including those of Enron

Corporation and WorldCom. Memories, though, proved short, and demand for CDOs soared as credit-rating cuts on corporate debt became rarer. (The economy was growing, and most companies had enough cash to cover their debts.) In 2004 and in Europe alone, Moody's rated $56 billion in collateralized debt backed by default swaps. That was a 20 percent gain over the previous year, according to figures provided by the company at the start of 2005.

By 2006, the global derivatives printing presses were stamping out $503 billion of collateralized debt for the ratings companies to grade, up from $274 billion in the previous year and $144 billion in 2004. In April 2007, Moody's announced a fourth-quarter profit increase of 20 percent, as revenue from rating structured finance transactions had leaped to $251.5 million, a 44 percent gain over the same period in 2006. Almost half of Moody's total 2007 sales of $583 million came from its structured notes business, dwarfing the $115 million it made by analyzing company creditworthiness.

Risk appetites increased, and CDOs became even more exotic and complicated. Structured product specialists worked to broaden their appeal by tying CDO values to a broader range of underlying markets; some even created theoretical bets that were tied to abstract prices.

To grade these new financial instruments, ratings companies used methodology that was fatally flawed from the start. It was based on induction: the process of inferring a general law or principle from the observation of particular instances. But the particular instances the ratings companies chose did not incorporate the lessons of previous housing booms, nor the nonexistent histories of some new, theoretical bets. Instead, ratings companies used the brief price history of the derivatives market as a benchmark to assess its likely future price performance.

Consider just one example. In the final quarter of 2004, Barclays Capital sought buyers willing to invest for five years in $15 million worth of CDOs, all tied to the prices of fifteen commodities, including precious metals such as gold, base metals such as copper, and energy commodities, including heating oil. Using derivatives called commodity trigger swaps, CDO buyers would make money—*unless* prices fell by 35 to 80 percent, depending on the commodity. S&P gave this transaction a "preliminary" AA assessment, placing the deal in the second-highest ratings band.

What kind of crystal ball let S&P judge the next 15 years of commodity prices with such certainty? The grading, the ratings company said in a November 2004 press release, was based on monthly price data since July 1973, used to run "the static portfolio through all the five-year periods covered by the data. For each five-year period, the number of triggers that would have been hit in the portfolio is determined. From this data, the historic probability distribution for the number of triggers is determined."

In other words, CDO ratings for this and other transactions were reliable, as long as the future turned out to be identical to the past. A different future, however, could make these ratings wildly inaccurate. The meteoric rise in U.S. house prices, vastly lower mortgage lending requirements, and the ensuing effect on the U.S. and global economies proved a combination that the markets had not seen before—and thus could not accurately predict.

When investors began to understand that they had been misled by credit ratings, protests ensued. In February 2005, HSH Nordbank, a Hamburg-based lender, sued U.K. bank Barclays saying that $151 million of collateralized-debt obligations it bought in 2000 "if saleable at all, have become worth a very great deal less." Pretrial documents included the allegation that Barclays had parked the money HSH put into its original purchase in a Barclays CDO issue called Taunton, which invested in a Barclays CDO named Flavius, which in turn took a stake in Barclays notes called Savannah II, which bought parts of two more CDO issues, Dorset and Tullas, created by (you guessed it) Barclays. (Investment bankers were getting better and better at recycling existing assets into new products.)

The collateralized debt that HSH purchased started life with ratings of AAA to BBB—all investment grade—from Fitch Ratings. By the time of the lawsuit, those ratings had deteriorated by at least nine levels, to between BBB– and CC. While an AAA security had an "exceptionally strong capacity for timely payment of financial commitments," according to Fitch's own definitions, the BBB– category was just one slip away from junk, while CC denoted "that default of some kind appears probable."

In February 2005, Barclays and HSH issued a joint press statement saying they'd reached a settlement. The terms of the accord weren't released; washing dirty CDO linen in public was a losing strategy for all concerned. The episode did make clear, though, that an AAA rating on a CDO was far from the seal of guaranteed quality it purported to be.

In May 2005, the derivatives market delivered a warning that anyone relying on mathematical models to predict the likely performance of structured credit investments during times of stress was asking for trouble. The warning, which most investors ignored, came from the auto industry.

Auto bonds were a useful source of collateral in the asset-backed debt market's growth, because U.S. carmakers used public debt markets voraciously to finance their businesses. When General Motors Corporation and Ford Motor Company lost their investment-grade ratings in May 2005, the downgrades ignited aftershocks of dislocation in the structured credit market—though not in the way that the theory of collateralized debt had predicted. In the price convulsions that followed downgrades, junk-rated CDO slices that had been built in part from automaker debt gained in value, while top-rated portions declined. That was completely counterintuitive, and went against everything that mathematical modeling had suggested might happen.

That turmoil should have alerted investors to the risk that market stresses could trigger unpredicted behavior in the derivatives arena. Nobody in finance, though, had any incentive to begin questioning the tools and techniques that were helping to make money for everybody in the CDO food chain. Most dismissed the episode as an aberration.

Risk—and Profits—from Thin Air

The derivatives engineers were confident in their ability to build a product to cover every eventuality, and a model that purported to predict the likelihood of each occurrence. Worried about a change in interest rates? Derivatives could make those dangers disappear. Indifferent to interest rates, but concerned about the health of a particular company? No problem—we can tailor a derivative that lets you sleep at night. Want to bet that a bunch of companies are in better shape than the market thinks they are? Here's an investment strategy customized to your particular paranoia and enthusiasm.

And derivative engineers weren't the only true believers. Regulators also bought into the belief that derivatives models accurately reflected market possibilities. Both groups completely missed the derivatives market's ability to fashion new risks out of nothing, allowing investors to send money on uncertain journeys purely for the fun of trying to make money—not to safeguard capital by alleviating a real, known hazard. The authorities convinced themselves that derivatives disseminated risk. Instead, buyers ran through a virtual fireworks factory, holding lighted blowtorches in each hand.

Credit-default swaps, for example, were created to let bondholders buy insurance against the possibility that a bond's issuer—the company using a bond to borrow money—might fail to make its payments. It was a reasonable product, something like car insurance: in case of an accident, the insurer pays you the value of your wrecked auto, so you can buy new wheels and still drive to work.

The banking community, however, exploited the product to the extreme. Banks began selling more insurance policies than there were cars, in essence, and investors who couldn't even drive began buying the contracts.

Suppose a company sold investors $100 million in bonds. Nothing prevented traders from basing $500 million of newly created credit-default swaps (CDSs) on those bonds, conjuring up five times as much risk as there really was.

A universe of virtual money blossomed into being. Bankers could print as many default swaps as they wanted, package them together into a CDO, and persuade investors to gamble on the creditworthiness of companies to which they hadn't lent any money. It's analogous to buying an insurance policy on a car you don't own, then selling that policy for more than you paid to someone else—someone who doesn't own a car either.

In the process, banks manufactured financial menace, rather than attempting to mitigate existing dangers. That became the principal activity hallmark of the derivatives industry, storing up trouble for the future.

The most egregious example of derivative market excess came with the invention of the Constant Proportion Debt Obligation, known as a CPDO. The idea had been knocking around for a few years—a July 2004 research note from Société Générale described a "Dynamic Portfolio Insurance" strategy that employed a similar approach—but it was the Dutch bank ABN Amro Holdings that first succeeded in harnessing the technique in a structure that clients would buy. In June 2006, ABN Amro issued a thirty-eight-page marketing brochure describing a security called "Surf—the First CPDO; a Breakthrough in Credit Investments."

CPDOs were the credit derivatives market's hottest alchemical method for transforming plumbous yield premiums into the gold of market-beating returns. The marketing literature and associated research reports suggested the newfangled securities were the holy grail of investing—heads you win, tails you don't lose.

CPDOs were an abstract bet on the likelihood of defaults in the corporate bond market. With their values tied to credit-default swap indexes, the securities promised to deliver as much as two percentage points more than money market rates during their ten-year life spans. That was worth about 5.6 percent at the three-month money market rates that prevailed when CPDOs began attracting attention in November 2006. At the time, German government debt, deemed the safest fixed-income investments in the European markets, yielded just 3.7 percent annually. No wonder CPDOs looked irresistible to investors.

Those remarkable rates of return were made possible by the magic of derivatives, which leveraged the initial bet by a multiplier of 15. CPDOs were like gamblers at a casino, doubling up when bets go awry by shifting chips from the safety of the pile to the danger of the baize. These gamblers, moreover, had to produce only one chip for the house to let them bet the equivalent of fifteen chips.

The leverage turned average punters into high rollers with the potential for fantastic gains—and losses. When times were good and a CPDO looked set to meet its payment obligations, sponsoring investment banks could reduce their market bets. When times got tougher, banks increased those wagers in an effort to boost the security's net asset value. Credit-rating companies issued CPDOs top ratings for both interest and principal payments.

In a famous financial market truism, everyone agrees there's no such thing as a free lunch—until, that is, they think that they alone have spotted a buffet of risk-free profit. CPDOs were too good to be true; they had the whiff of a Nigerian banking scam, in which the sales director of the Democratic Republic of Derivatives offers a crack at millions of dollars hidden in an unexplored corner of the Republic in the form of Constant Proportion Debt Obligations, or CPDOs, based on nothing more than anonymous assurances of "your honesty and integrity for an Urgent Business Proposal in Confidence of the Strictest Nature."

Dislocation's Aftershocks

By November 2007, Moody's was telling investors it might cut the Aaa ratings on two of ABN's CPDOs, along with five CPDOs and one swap contract initiated by Swiss investment bank UBS and rated between Aaa and Aa3.

One of the ABN CPDOs, called Chess III, had gone on sale in July 2007, its golden Aaa rating supporting its price: 100 percent of face value. Just four months later, it was worth about 41.5 percent of face value, according to ABN's own prices. Put another way, investors who bought the €100 million ($147 million) in notes lost €58.5 million in just sixteen weeks. They might have done better in a Nigerian e-mail fraud.

In July 2008, Moody's fired the head of its structured finance unit after finding that a computer error produced overly generous Aaa ratings on at least $4 billion of CPDOs. The *Financial Times* reported that the mistake had inflated grades by as many as four levels. The life of the CPDO market was nasty, brutish, and short: the product survived for just one year.

As it turned out, buyers who trusted CPDO and CDO creators— and even the most sophisticated derivatives purchasers had to place some reliance on what sellers' stress-testing models suggested about future valuations—misplaced their faith. Let down once by sellers, buyers were also betrayed by ratings companies. "It could be structured by cows and we would rate it," S&P analyst Shannon Mooney told a colleague in April 2007 in an e-mail uncovered by a U.S. Congress committee in an October 2008 investigation into ratings companies' role in the unfolding credit crisis.

By the middle of 2007, investors were asking how many beans make four in the CDO market. The answer, to their dismay, was three if you're lucky, and fewer if you're not. They had paid little attention to CDOs' buried contents and were ignorant of the role their uninformed choices had played in underwriting the subprime mortgage surge.

The consequences continued to play out. In the second week of July 2007, Moody's cut ratings on $5.2 billion in bonds backed by subprime home loans and put a further $5 billion in CDOs on review. S&P lowered its assessment of $6.39 billion in debt. It was the start of the CDO market's unraveling.

The freewheeling mortgage market of 2006, when home buyers could borrow from lenders who had no economic reason to care whether the loans would be repaid, destroyed any ability the ratings companies had to predict likely delinquency or default rates on CDOs that were tied to the subprime mortgage market. Mehernosh Engineer, a London-based credit strategist at the French bank BNP Paribas, called on ratings companies to abandon the pretense. "Their models are basically unable to predict any 'normal' behavior due to this overriding fraud factor," Engineer wrote in a research report published in July 2007. "The right thing for the rating agencies to do for the 2006 vintage would be to withdraw all ratings."

The alphabet soup cooked up by the derivatives chefs—boil some CDOs, toss in a dash of ABS and a soupçon of CDS, season with CPDOs, and serve with a garnish of overly optimistic ratings— was sufficiently toxic to poison the entire financial system. Capitalism itself ended up looking sickly and anemic. Belatedly, investors discovered the truth of one of billionaire investor Warren Buffett's aphorisms: unraveling a derivatives trade, the so-called Oracle of Omaha had said, was like trying to carry "a cat home by its tail."

Wall Street had invented a machine that could recycle just about anything that generated a cash flow. It had a growing, reliable source of supply from the housing market, sufficient to keep the merry-go-round spinning. And shifts in both the investment banking culture and the investing landscape created a willing coalition of buyers and sellers.

THREE

Priced for Perfection

The Financial Gene Pool Economic Darwinism Couldn't Improve

The development of economic systems which concentrate on the common good depends on a determinate ethical system. The decline of such discipline can actually cause the laws of the market to collapse. We need a maximum of specialized economic understanding, but also a maximum of ethos so that specialized economic understanding may enter the service of the right goals.

— POPE BENEDICT XVI, APRIL 2005

FEAR AND GREED TYPICALLY DRIVE securities markets, and losing money is a sure-fire way that traders learn to balance those two conflicting emotions.

By the end of 2006, though, it was as if market losses had become historical oddities, something your parents or grandparents had endured in sepia-tinged times. Fear had been vanquished; greed was pervasive, all-powerful, and busily destroying any lingering inhibitions the financial community might have had about how much collective risk it would accumulate in chasing gains. Economic Darwinism

41

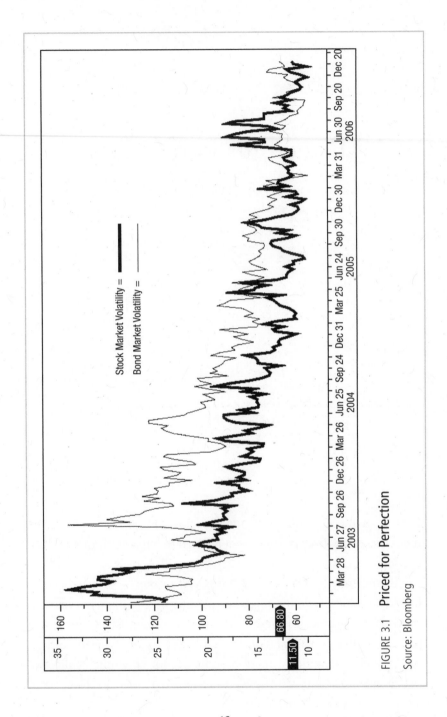

FIGURE 3.1 Priced for Perfection

Source: Bloomberg

wasn't working as it should. The least fit weren't just surviving, they were prospering, to the gene pool's ultimate detriment. The ubiquitous bull market bred complacency, erasing the need for discrimination and caution. As the credit boom gathered pace, a kind of reckless hedonism gripped the world's securities markets.

Warnings at Davos

When more than 2,500 of the world's business leaders gathered in January 2007 for the annual World Economic Forum in Davos, Switzerland, the global capital markets appeared to have achieved something like nirvana. U.S. government bond futures contracts had climbed 6 percent in the previous six months, suggesting that debt market participants were confident of a bright future. The Standard & Poor's 500 Index of the leading U.S. stocks had surged 14 percent in the same period, so life for players in the equity markets was also looking good. Gold, meanwhile, ended 2006 trading at $637 per ounce, a gain of more than 20 percent in a year. Real estate values continued their relentless climb.

In traders' parlance, all markets were priced for perfection, a situation in which security values rely on everything turning out as expected, with no alarms and no surprises. Alarms and surprises at any point, on the other hand, would inevitably weaken the entire frame-work, because the global financial web was so closely interwoven. This helps explain the speed at which the credit boom gathered force and the severity with which it exploded.

It does little, however, to explain why the three markets—debt, equity, and gold—were simultaneously optimistic. It was a bit like backing every horse in a race: you're assured of picking the winner, but the odds mean you'll lose your shirt to the bookmakers.

Bond values typically increase when slowing economic growth curbs inflation and central banks cut interest rates to stimulate spending and demand. In that environment, the regular interest payments generated by loans to governments and companies become more valuable, and debt becomes a more attractive purchase.

Equities, meanwhile, are more in vogue when economic growth is fast enough to bolster company profits, boosting the prospect of higher stock dividend payments. And rising gold prices, conventional wisdom says, flash a warning sign that investors are concerned about faster inflation and seek a safe haven for their savings. Now all three markets were simultaneously optimistic. Something strange was happening.

Financial Nirvana

Music producers joke that the most successful heavy metal records are those in which every instrument is louder than every other instrument. A global capital market in which everything was becoming more expensive than everything else was a market that was cruising for a bruising. To bankers who paid themselves multimillion-dollar bonuses, this felt like nirvana. Perhaps it wasn't the nirvana characterized by nonattachment to material things—there were those bonuses, after all—but the parallel gains in market prices suggested that traders and investors had extinguished their attachment to economic theory.

"One would expect gold and the debt market to move in contravention, for strong gold means rising inflation which is, of course, anathema to debt investments," Dennis Gartman, an economist who publishes a daily market commentary called *The Gartman Letter*, told his subscribers in December 2006. "The only reason we can ascertain to push both higher is weakening economic environs, deflation and serious economic dislocations."

Gartman, who is based in Suffolk, Virginia, has a collection of mantras he suggests clients use to help guide their trading decisions. "Buy when they're cryin', sell when they're yellin'," is one. "Do more of that which is working and do less of that which is not," is another.

At a time when everything seemed to be working, however, it was tough to come up with concrete, rational arguments for taking a contrarian, bearish view on any asset class. "Sellin' when they're yellin'" looked like a ticket to unemployment when all markets seemed to be gaining simultaneously. The investment world was swept along on a tide of euphoria and boundless optimism, forgetting one of the most basic lessons that traders are supposed to learn by heart: when everyone leans in the same direction, it's the best time to question the prevailing orthodoxy.

Prices for bonds, stocks, gold, and property were all climbing higher at a time when economists were increasingly divided on the prospects for growth and inflation in the United States the world's largest economy. Bloomberg News surveyed more than 60 economists in August 2006 about the outlook for the end of the year. According to the bleakest predictions, the United States looked set to flounder at a quarterly annualized growth rate of 1.4 percent. Consumer prices would decline by 1.9 percent, the Federal Reserve's overnight lending rate target would drop to 4.5 percent from 5.25 percent, and the 10 year Treasury bond would yield 4.25 percent.

The most optimistic forecasts in the same survey, though, painted an alternative scenario in which growth surged to 4.1 percent by December, inflation accelerated to 4.2 percent, the Fed funds rate climbed to 6 percent, and 10 year Treasuries yielded 5.85 percent.

Even with a nod to the old joke about laying 1,000 economists end-to-end and still not reaching a conclusion, the survey highlighted an unusually wide difference of opinion. It suggested a potential swing of 2.7 percentage points in between the best and worst projected outcomes for growth, with inflation forecasts diverging by 6.1 points. Depending which crystal ball you favored, a case could be made for preferring the dependable interest income from bonds, the long-term growth potential of stocks, *and* the safe haven of gold.

Ambiguities and disagreements about the economic outlook polluted the atmosphere at the Federal Reserve's annual brainstorming session for central bankers and economists in August 2006 in Jackson Hole, Wyoming. Mickey Levy, who attended the meeting as the chief economist for New York's Bank of America Corporation, said afterward that "great uncertainty about how the decline in housing will affect the consumer, tremendous uncertainty about the outlook for capital spending, and just uncertainty" were the summit's overriding themes.

The central banks responsible for steering global monetary policy were even less sure than usual about the economic outlook, so money managers should have adopted defensive strategies designed to preserve capital in a wide variety of potential tomorrows. Sometimes the sidelines are the wisest place to be, as well as the safest. As the bull markets roared ahead, however, no one wanted to play it safe and risk being left behind.

The Hedge Fund Bogeyman

In September 2006, another unheeded warning bell sounded in the financial markets. A hedge fund called Amaranth Advisors, a second-tier player that even at its peak managed just $9.2 billion, went bust after trader Brian Hunter made bad bets on the price of natural gas. The fund lost $4.6 billion in a single week and multiplied the deficit to $6.6 billion by the end of that month. Hunter's decisions left the fund crippled by a 60 percent loss for the year.

Hedge funds are the bogeymen of finance, arousing a morbid fascination among professional and amateur market watchers alike. These funds, which have earned a reputation for combining great secrecy with the promise of high pay for managers and high returns for clients, are lightly regulated investment vehicles.

Despite that light regulation, hedge funds may have the potential to cause substantial problems in the broader market if and when their bets go wrong. The 1998 implosion of Long-Term Capital

Management LP, a hedge fund that counted Nobel Prize winners among its founding fathers, had threatened to unravel the entire financial system. (That, at least, that was what the Federal Reserve suggested when it twisted Wall Street's arms in an effort to bail out LTCM.)

Restricted to managing money for wealthy clients, most hedge funds say they make money whether markets go up or down. (They claim to do this through futures and other derivative instruments that allow them to gamble on the prices of things they don't own.) Their managers are among the best paid of all financial professionals. A typical hedge fund takes 2 percent of assets under management and hangs on to 20 percent of any profit it generates.

Hedge funds' proliferation helped stoke the credit boom by hatching a new, timely crop of buyers to soak up the profusion of derivatives the investment banks busily spawned. Clients lined up to hand money to hedge funds, lured by the promise of superior returns. For their part, the hedge funds were eager to amass the most complicated products on offer, attempting to justify their fees by delivering top returns. And the investment banks happily lent hedge funds the money they needed to multiply their bets, in return for a chance to handle their trades and stock their investment warehouses. Everyone's interests, it seemed, were aligned.

When the story of Amaranth's collapse broke, it swiftly became the most-read article ever on the Bloomberg News service. Its popularity among an audience of financial professionals was clear evidence that even market experts felt an underlying nervousness about the secretive trading strategies that the hedge funds used to bolster their profits. (The previous record for the most-viewed story had been set in November 2001, when news about a New York plane crash fueled concern over a potential repeat of the September 11 terrorist attacks that destroyed the World Trade Center.)

Schadenfreude—that wonderful German expression denoting malicious enjoyment of others' misfortunes—also helped stoke curiosity about Amaranth's demise. Though few had heard of the company, investment bankers enjoyed hearing bad news about a market segment that many envied.

Traders at some top-drawer investment banks, such as Goldman Sachs, Deutsche Bank, or Morgan Stanley, didn't necessarily earn any less than their freewheeling peers at hedge fund clusters in Connecticut and London. Even so, they often envied hedge fund traders, who seemed more in control of their own workday destinies. Around the time Amaranth exploded, a friend told me she might join a hedge fund, just to choose which brand of coffee she'd drink at the office each day.

By providing a viable alternative career route for financial professionals brave enough to consider life outside an investment bank's cozy embrace, hedge funds helped inflate salaries across the board in finance. It was another of those win-win situations that the world of money specialized in creating: join a hedge fund for more money and freedom, or stay at an investment bank and get a bigger bonus, one that will persuade you not to join a hedge fund.

Rubbernecking at Amaranth's crash was a spectator sport. It didn't occur to the onlookers, though, to wonder whether the mathematical models they relied on to test the safety of their *own* trading strategies might be just as flawed as the smoke detectors that had failed to warn Amaranth of impending financial asphyxiation.

Investors plowed $42.1 billion into hedge funds in the second quarter of 2006, the most they had allocated in a three-month period since at least 2003, according to figures compiled by Chicago's Hedge Fund Research. By the time Amaranth blew up, the hedge fund industry was toying with $1.2 trillion. It wasn't just wealthy individuals who were seduced by the promise of elephantine returns. Organizations of all sorts, from university endowment funds to local government pension committees, invested money with hedge funds. They wanted ever-higher returns, but had little understanding of where their cash was romping off to play.

By 2004, however, those ever-higher returns were waning. Hedge fund profits declined, partly because newer hedge funds were less skillful than their predecessors, and partly because the market suffered from what investors call crowded trades. When everyone made the same bets, profitability dropped.

Hedge fund customers enjoyed returns of more than 15 percent in 2003, but got less than 10 percent in 2004 and about 7.6 percent in 2005, according to figures compiled by Credit Suisse Group and Tremont Capital Management. In 2006 hedge fund returns rebounded to almost 14 percent—but investors would have done better with a simple stock market index-tracking fund that year. Including reinvested dividends, the S&P 500 Index gained almost 16 percent in 2006, as did the Russell 3000 Index. The Dow Jones Industrial Average returned more than 19 percent, while the Dow Jones Stoxx 600 index of leading European stocks delivered almost 18 percent.

Industry rules, moreover, made it hard to be sure just how much money hedge funds were making. Firstly, all disclosure was voluntary; hedge funds weren't obliged to tell anyone except their clients how well—or how badly—they were doing. It seemed reasonable to assume, therefore, that only the better-performing funds submitted numbers to the various research firms trying to keep tabs on the industry. The laggards would stay silent, making for skewed data and overall results that looked better than they actually were.

The second, related shortcoming concerned a phenomenon known as survivor bias. Hedge fund data only included investors who managed to stay in the game. Those who fell by the wayside also left the data pool, without reporting their disasters.

These reporting flaws were well known, but didn't slow the hedge fund industry's breakneck growth. In 2006, a record $127 billion flowed into hedge funds, boosting the total assets they managed to $1.5 trillion, according to figures compiled by Chicago-based analysis firm Hedge Fund Research. The market had more than doubled in just four years, and had taken just ten years to grow sixfold. The hedge fund universe peaked in 2007, with $1.9 trillion in investments.

Every time authorities considered tightening hedge fund oversight, the financial community lobbied successfully for the status quo. After all, investors wanted unbelievably high returns—and weren't about to let believability get in their way. What's more, Wall Street had built a lucrative derivatives machine, and hedge funds were a key customer. More oversight was not in the market's best interest.

Volatility Disappears

Simultaneous gains in stocks, bonds, and gold hinted that too much money—and leverage—were chasing ever-diminishing returns. "The amount of leverage in the system is growing at rates that are scary," Nouriel Roubini, professor of economics at the Stern School of Business, New York University, told his peers at the January 2007 Davos gathering. "The risk of something systemic happening is rising."

Roubini wasn't the only Davos delegate that year to voice fears about the potential consequences of a mishap in the global financial markets. Bank of China Vice President Zhu Min told a panel discussion that "we really don't know what the risks are" of a clear surge in global liquidity. Vittorio Corbo, head of Chile's central bank, described the prevailing economic and financial conditions at the beginning of 2007 as "too good to be true."

In the worlds of commerce and finance, however, such warnings went unheeded. The consultant firm PricewaterhouseCoopers publishes an annual survey timed to coincide with the Davos summit; in 2007, 92 percent of the 1,084 respondents said they were "confident" or "very confident" about the economic outlook. That was the highest positive response the firm had recorded since introducing the study a decade earlier.

Stocks, bonds, and gold weren't the only investments that ended 2006 in a bullish mood. Just about every barometer of market risk suggested that conditions had never been better and could only improve.

The markets began to eschew even short-term dips in value. The VIX index, a measure of U.S. stock market volatility that's calculated by the Chicago Board Options Exchange, dropped below 10 in December 2006 for the first time since 1993. Its average value was 13 in 2005, 15.5 in 2004, 22 in 2003, and 27 in 2002. In effect, the VIX index suggested that equity markets were at their most stable in more than a decade.

The bond markets were more stable, too. At the end of 2006, traders and investors expected Treasury bond prices to swing by just 0.57 percentage points in the next twelve months, according to Merrill Lynch's MOVE index, which tracks bond options prices to gauge likely future price changes. The MOVE index had an average value of 0.67 in the first half of 2006, 0.79 in the previous year, 0.99 in 2004, and more than 1.13 in 2003. In short, market expectations for bond price volatility declined by half in just three years. "The bond market has a worrying degree of confidence in global policy makers," Dario Perkins, a European economist at ABN Amro in London, warned his clients in August 2006 in a research report. "Speak to any central banker and they are not so sanguine—they know they will make mistakes."

Central banks did try to damp down expectations, but in terms that, in retrospect, were much too mild. In May 2006, for example, Paul Tucker, the Bank of England's executive director with responsibility for financial markets, told a conference that the explosive growth in derivatives designed to slice and dice risk might make it harder for investors to work out how exposed they were to market shifts. Recent developments "make it difficult for market participants to assess and price for how much risk there is," Tucker told a gathering of the Association of Corporate Treasurers in Wales.

A month later his boss, Mervyn King, said policy makers should "recognize that we've been through the fastest three-year period of growth in the world economy for a generation. It would be unreasonable to expect the world economy to grow quite as rapidly in the next three years as it has done in the past three."

Risk and Reward: A Relationship Comes Apart

When prices flatline, traders struggle to make money. Skillful traders don't care whether values rise or decline, so long as the fluctuations occur in a range that's wide enough to create meaningful differences between buying and selling prices. An environment of receding volatility forces a bonus-conscious trader to take wilder gambles in pursuit of profit.

Mainstream markets weren't alone in seeing higher prices and lower volatility. Emerging markets had always been one of the racier corners of the trading universe, offering above-average returns to those who accepted the risk of investing in countries with less developed economies.

By the end of 2006, though, it was as if the likes of Brazil, Mexico, and Russia had never defaulted on their obligations. Collectively, emerging market nations paid an average of 1.7 percentage points more for their money than the U.S. government did that year, according to a debt index maintained by JPMorgan Chase & Co. The premium hovered above 4 percentage points just two years earlier, and surpassed 10 percentage points in the third quarter of 2002. Emerging market debt was one-fifth as lucrative as it had been four years earlier. Put another way, traders were treating it as if it were 80 percent less risky.

Investors don't lend money to Poland, Venezuela, or Vietnam because the nations are interesting holiday destinations; they do it to earn a higher return on clients' money, taking the extra compensation developing countries offer to investors who forgo the economic safety and political stability of the United States or Germany. As monetary incentives diminish, such bonds should become less popular. Instead, money managers awash with cash continued to pile into these deals, driving yields ever lower.

In its 2007 annual report, the Bank for International Settlements gave a stark warning about how the feedback loop between the intermingled, rising markets might snap. "There seems to be a natural tendency in markets for past successes to lead to more risk-taking, more leverage, more funding, higher prices, more collateral and, in turn, more risk-taking," the BIS report authors wrote. "The danger with such endogenous market processes is that they can, indeed must, eventually go into reverse if the fundamentals have been overpriced. Moreover, should liquidity dry up, and correlations among asset prices rise, the concern would be that prices might also overshoot on the downside."

House Prices Stumble

While the world's financial markets enjoyed unbridled optimism, the profligate, incautious lending policies of the preceding years were coming home to roost in the U.S. housing market. The rot of bad lending decisions was starting to eat away at the insubstantial foundations of finance's halcyon days.

In the final quarter of 2006, 4.95 percent of U.S. mortgage holders failed to make payments. That was the highest delinquency level in three years, according to figures compiled by the Mortgage Bankers Association of America.

Picture a street of one hundred houses in Anywhere, America. By the end of 2006, every twentieth household couldn't make its mortgage payments. Perhaps an introductory low-interest period on the loan had ended and the monthly payments had soared, yet the home's value had dropped too far to allow refinancing—the owners' original plan. Or perhaps the owners simply lacked the income they would have needed to sustain mortgage payments. In either case, imagine the stress, misery, and anxiety each homeowner felt.

Among the riskier subprime lenders, the delinquency rate climbed to a four-year high of 13.33 percent. On another street in America, every seventh household had stopped paying its mortgage.

Nevertheless, Brian Coulton, head of global economics at Fitch Ratings in London, wrote in a January 2007 research report that the economy was at minimal risk from leveled or decreasing housing prices. "U.S. house price inflation is likely to fall close to zero in coming quarters," Coulton estimated. "This implies real house price declines in 2007 and 2008, but not on the scale witnessed in previous housing market troughs in the early 1980s and 1990s. The avoidance of significant price declines would help reduce the risks of a sharp and sustained retrenchment in U.S. consumer spending and underpin Fitch's expectations of a 'soft landing' for the U.S. economy," Coulton wrote. Coulton should have paid more attention to the history of the global housing market.

As U.S. Democratic Congressman Barney Frank told the *New Yorker* magazine in its January 12, 2009, edition, "There are people in this society who don't have enough money to be homeowners, and there are people whose lives are not sufficiently integrated for them to take on the responsibility to be a homeowner. And we did too much pushing of people into inappropriate mortgages and into homeownership."

An Illusory Nirvana

The drive to turn all renters into owners had practical consequences. By the end of 2006, lenders had foreclosed on properties backed by 1.19 percent of the total residential loans outstanding, the highest percentage since the first quarter of 2004.

Those defaulting loans were woven throughout the securities industry. To ensure that the merry-go-round kept spinning, the investment banks hadn't just waited for the housing market to generate subprime mortgages for repackaging; instead, the banks had bought mortgage lenders themselves, getting in on the ground floor.

HSBC Holdings, Britain's biggest bank, paid $15.5 billion for subprime lender Household International in 2003. In May 2006, Wachovia, then the fourth biggest bank in the U.S., paid almost $25 billion for Golden West Financial. Golden West's specialty was in designing option adjustable rate mortgages, which allow borrowers to defer part of their regular interest payments and instead add the unpaid portion to loan principal. At the tail end of the credit boom in late 2006, Merrill Lynch paid $1.3 billion for a company called First Franklin, which specialized in channelling loans to people with weak credit scores.

The banks weren't particularly interested in the mortgage business for its own sake. Dealing with credit checks, appraisals, and job and income verification held little charm. Banks did, however, have substantial profits at stake in assembling those lucrative collateralized-debt obligations (CDOs). Owning a subprime mortgage company gave a bank direct access to the raw ingredients needed to keep the CDO vats bubbling, ensuring that the pipeline never ran dry.

Banks were able to position themselves on every step of the CDO supply staircase. They owned the lenders that granted the mortgages, fermented those home loans via the credit-rating companies, and brewed batches of new CDOs to sell in the derivatives marketplace.

As more and more of those mortgages failed, they began to unravel finance's already weakened fabric.

Borrowers began to lose their houses, and the mortgage debt that had been endlessly recycled through the financial markets was beginning to disintegrate. Financial nirvana was proving to be a temporary illusion—one brought on by mass financial hysteria.

FOUR

Bubbles, Bubbles Everywhere

Global Liquidity's Search for a Profitable Home

*The United States is dreaming if it thought the 21st Century was the
American century.*

> —Former Chinese Vice Premier Qian Qichen,
> cited in the official *China Daily* newspaper's
> online edition in November 2004

In early 2007, Jeremy Grantham, the chairman of a Boston-based
investment company called Grantham, Mayo, Van Otterloo &
Company, suggested that the world was witnessing "the first truly
global bubble." In his widely distributed newsletter, Grantham made
a list: "From Indian antiquities to modern Chinese art; from land in
Panama to Mayfair; from forestry, infrastructure and the junkiest
bonds to mundane blue chips—it's bubble time."

With the world seemingly awash with money, China played a
vital—if somewhat inadvertent—two-part role in shaping the economic landscape in which the credit boom blossomed. As expanding
trade links integrated the nation of 1.3 billion people more fully with

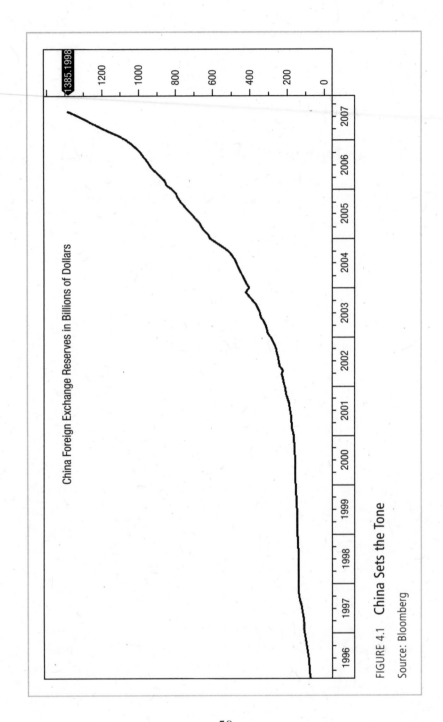

China Foreign Exchange Reserves in Billions of Dollars

FIGURE 4.1 China Sets the Tone

Source: Bloomberg

the rest of the world, China's increasingly visible, active presence on the commercial stage bestowed two economic gifts on Western countries. These gifts carried deceptively complex consequences.

The China Syndrome

Firstly, China inundated the world with cheap goods, driving down the prices of everything from textiles to electronic products. That, in turn, suppressed global consumer price inflation, almost to the point of extinction. Many rural Chinese residents abandoned subsistence farming and swarmed into the nation's manufacturing centers. In doing so, they inflicted a massive, unprecedented supply shock on the mercantile realm, which then rippled through the world of finance in a series of connected waves.

As global consumer goods prices dropped, central banks grew more and more comfortable maintaining low monetary policy rates. Lower policy rates meant less expensive credit, making it easier to borrow money and play the financial markets. More cheap money in the markets meant lower potential profits—*except* that the flood of cheap money also drove down volatility, which made everyone more relaxed about making riskier and riskier bets.

This was one of the weirder consequences of the world's rapid globalization. Commerce and finance intertwined and encircled the globe, knitting intimate connections between unlikely nodes. The big city seduces a young Chinese farmer, who quits his village to sew t-shirts in a factory. Not too many steps along the causal chain later, a hedge fund manager in Manhattan makes credit-default swap market bets at prices he would never have entertained a year earlier.

China's second contribution to the credit boom intensified those financial repercussions. China had both a burgeoning trade surplus and an official policy of controlling the value of its currency on the foreign exchange markets. That gave the state authorities massive financial firepower in the form of cash that could be recycled into the global financial markets to generate apparently infinite liquidity.

China's idiosyncratic, home-grown brand of tightly controlled capitalism allowed a thousand entrepreneurial flowers to bloom, energizing the economy. In the ten years before the end of 2006, China's economy grew at an average quarterly pace of 8.6 percent, almost three times as fast as the U.S. economy during the same period. That in turn put upward pressure on China's currency, the yuan, which Chinese authorities resisted for fear that a stronger currency would inhibit export growth by making Chinese goods more expensive for overseas buyers.

China's solution was to sell yuan and buy U.S. dollars, building the nation's stockpile of foreign exchange reserves to more than $1 trillion by October 2006, up from just $155 billion at the start of the decade. In the capitalist spirit of the times, China didn't just stuff that growing mountain of dollars underneath its mattress. It invested the cash.

Lending to Uncle Sam

Some of that cash bought U.S. government bonds. By the first quarter of 2000, China had lent Uncle Sam $72 billion by buying Treasury bonds, according to estimates compiled by the U.S. Treasury. By the first quarter of 2007, China's U.S. debt purchases had soared six-fold, to $420 billion. China also bought higher-yielding securities it deemed as safe as Treasuries: mortgage-backed bonds from Fannie Mae and Freddie Mac, two government-sponsored mortgage repurchasers whose role it is to broaden the availability of mortgages to U.S. homeowners.

Fannie and Freddie bonds had implicit U.S. government backing, though not an explicit guarantee. Despite that ambiguous distinction, the market was confident that U.S. authorities would never allow either company to default on its debt. Between June 2003 and June 2006, China increased its ownership of U.S. mortgage-backed securities from just $3 billion to $107.5 billion, according to figures compiled by the U.S. Department of Housing and Urban Development. China bought debt offered by Fannie and Freddie, as well as securities sold by Ginnie Mae, a third U.S. agency that did have the U.S. government's explicit guarantee.

Here was another of globalization's odd consequences. A college kid in Connecticut buys a cheap cotton t-shirt sewed by a young ex-farmer in China. That purchase funnels money into the Chinese government's coffers. China uses that cash to buy mortgage-backed debt, fanning the flames of the overheated U.S. property market.

To policy makers in the United States and Europe, it looked like another win-win situation. Inflation was vanquished, which went a long way toward satisfying their desire for economic stability. China was helping to pay for the borrowing that helped fund the American dream. Money was cheap, which kept economic growth humming along. And all the time, the authorities remained blissfully ignorant of how the financial community was making the most of this remarkable investment climate.

With volatility near flat and yield premiums shrinking on even the least appetizing flavors of nongovernment debt, money managers had to make riskier bets to keep returns high or lose their customers to someone who was willing to play faster and looser.

When more than a thousand financial world participants met for Europe's biggest annual bond symposium on February 27, 2007, in London's Queen Elizabeth II Conference Centre they focused on making the most of the good times, not on what might go wrong. The atmosphere was thick with complacency, even though the week had begun with former Federal Reserve Chairman Alan Greenspan warning that there was a chance that the United States might slip into recession later in the year.

Mark Johnson, who was hosting the event in his role as Euromoney Institutional Investor's conferences editor, tried to cajole guests into revealing their secret fears. Mark Brett, a portfolio manager at Los Angeles–based investment firm Capital Research & Management Company, said he was less concerned about the likelihood of a market collapse than he was about the prospect that regulators could overreact to any declines by tightening the rules governing financial firms.

"People are frustrated with how much risk you can get into a portfolio," offered Maria Ryan, the senior fixed-income strategist at Barclays Global Investors in London. "We do want volatility back in the market."

Be Careful What You Wish For

The night before the conference opened, the Chinese stock market suffered a crisis of confidence. The Shanghai Composite Index shed almost 9 percent in a single trading session, its steepest decline in a decade. The drop followed Chinese authorities' latest attempt to cool the investment exuberance that more than doubled the value of the Shanghai Index in 2006; the Chinese said investor excitement helped overheat the economy. To cool it, the government created a task force to investigate whether investors used personal loans to buy shares, which was illegal under China's securities laws.

Investors who owned Chinese stocks took fright. It wasn't the enforcement of existing domestic laws that triggered the panic, though—it was the prospect of China's regulators becoming increasingly vigilant about the activities of foreign investors, potentially blocking their access to one of the world's hottest stock markets.

As the London conference progressed, more and more of the delegates retreated to the corners, tapping on Blackberries and muttering into mobile telephones. The Dow Jones index of the leading

600 European stocks shed 3 percent of its value. The iTraxx Crossover Index of European credit-default swaps had its worst two days since the birth of the credit derivatives market. The VIX index, the Chicago exchange's measure of expected U.S. stock market volatility, was about to post its biggest one-day jump ever; the U.S. stock market was heading into its worst week in four years. Suddenly, the smart money gathered in the conference center wasn't quite so sure of itself.

By day two of the conference, the scale of market carnage was clear. The speakers who opened proceedings on February 28 were subdued. "There's a lot more potential downside than upside in credit; when the proverbial hits the fan, everything gets hit," said Michael Perotti, chief investment officer of Union Bancaire Privée.

"We're not getting paid for taking risk," said Louis Gargour, chief investment officer of LNG Capital. "I don't know why so many people are still buying credit."

At the marketing stands outside the main conference hall, attendees stopped collecting the free umbrellas, Hacky Sacks, and stress balls on offer from exhibitors. Instead, they clustered around a Bloomberg television screen to listen to Fed Chairman Ben Bernanke, who had just taken over from Alan Greenspan, reassure the world that financial markets were "working well." Even without the benefit of hindsight, his comments came across as overly complacent.

In retrospect, the most prescient comment at the gathering came from Melanie Owen, a London-based portfolio manager in Goldman Sachs' asset management unit. In a panel discussion, she wondered aloud what might happen if credit ratings deteriorated on the $796 billion of collateralized-debt obligations sold in the previous year, prompting a flood of investors to try selling damaged CDOs, all at the same time. "What does this volume of money do when it exits?" she asked. Just as the 1987 stock market crash laid bare the shortcomings of computer-controlled equity trading strategies, so the credit crunch would eventually expose the derivative market's liquidity defects.

At the time, though, Owen's query was merely hypothetical. Most of the conference speakers were convinced that financial markets had become self-correcting mechanisms, with new money always available to bolster prices. "Hedge funds prevent prices from moving too far away from their equilibrium value," George Hoguet, the global investment strategist at Boston-based State Street Global Advisors, told the conference. The derivatives industry, meanwhile, was always there to take advantage of slipping values, and was poised to "jump in as spreads widen," according to Joe Biernat, head of research at European Credit Management Ltd.

Such attitudes proved fatally hubristic. Sure, liquidity was freely available when prices were stable or rising, but it could disappear almost instantly when prices faltered. A hiccup in the Chinese stock market caused short-lived havoc in the world's financial centers, a fact that should have served as a warning about just how interconnected the system had become, and how flimsy its underpinnings might prove if investors' underlying confidence faltered. But because the panic was hard to explain, market participants ignored it, dismissing the ripples as an aberration, much as they had ignored derivatives market turmoil a few years earlier, when General Motors and Ford suffered credit rating downgrades. Traders and investors were in thrall to their computer models, disregarding market moves that didn't fit electronic predictions.

Popping Risk Kernels

Meanwhile, in the U.S. housing market, the situation was quickly deteriorating. By the end of the first quarter of 2007, almost 14 percent of U.S. mortgage holders were at least thirty days in arrears, according to figures compiled by the Mortgage Bankers Association.

U.S. banks suffered from the results, of course, but so did overseas lenders. Britain's HSBC was the biggest player in the U.S.

subprime market, a result of buying Household International in 2003. In March 2007, HSBC said that its North American bad loans had climbed by more than 50 percent to $4.6 billion in 2006, and that it was setting aside $10.6 billion against losses in its worldwide lending business. (At the time, that seemed like an awful lot of money.)

HSBC's losses illustrated the housing downturn's severity and also showed how a bank's far-flung operations could be difficult to oversee and manage, yet still torpedo profit from thousands of miles away. The U.S. subprime market, HSBC warned, was "unstable" and in a "downturn." As its losses mounted, HSBC said it planned to "run down significantly" its U.S. mortgage lending business.

Economists often use letters of the alphabet to illustrate where they think an economy is headed. A "V," for example, suggests growth will decline and then rally; an "L" shape, by contrast, suggests an economic collapse that flatlines without rebounding. "A lot of people are looking for a 'V' in this recovery," Paul Puryear, the head of real estate research at Raymond James & Associates in St. Petersburg, Florida, said in a Bloomberg Television interview broadcast on March 12, 2007. "We've had a very quick downturn, and I think a lot of people think we are going to have a quick upturn. We just don't see how that can happen. We expect an 'L'".

In a report issued during the same month, analysts at Lehman Brothers Holdings estimated that defaults in the $8.5 trillion U.S. mortgage market could climb to $225 billion in the following two years, up from about $40 billion annually in 2005 and 2006. About $170 billion of that would come from lender defaults in the $1.2 trillion subprime market, according to the Lehman report. Ken Rosen, an economist at the University of California, Berkeley, predicted that 1.5 million of the 80 million U.S. homeowners could lose their properties to foreclosure during the coming downturn.

At Merrill Lynch, chief U.S. strategist Richard Bernstein was concerned that the markets had overlooked a series of financial warning signs. "The analogy we like to use to represent growing risk is one of popcorn popping in a microwave oven," Bernstein wrote in an April 2007 research report. "Each kernel that pops is an independent event, yet eventually the bag is full of popcorn. The major events that investors remember from history typically occur when the popcorn bag is full."

Bernstein identified eight generally ignored events that should have pinged radar screens around the investment community. He listed the collapse of hedge fund Amaranth in September; Venezuela's April 2007 threat to nationalize private health-care clinics thought to be overcharging patients; Ecuador's February 2007 warning that it might default on $10 billion of foreign debt; evidence of what Bernstein called a "bear market" in some commodities; Thailand's bungled capital controls, which were designed to limit rules on foreign ownership of domestic companies; the increase in bankruptcies in the U.S. subprime mortgage market; the United States' March 2007 decision to impose trade tariffs on coated paper from government-subsidized Chinese companies; and India's surprise decision in April 2007 to raise interest rates.

"Risk typically manifests itself within the financial markets not as a big single event, but rather as a series of small events that generally go ignored," Bernstein wrote. "The best way to manage portfolios is to marginally turn down the risk profile of the portfolio every time a kernel pops."

Money Moves to Private Equity

Perversely, the subprime mortgage market's collapse—and the diminishing value of investments associated with it—did very little to erode investors' appetite for risk. Instead of turning down the risk profile, traders steered money that might previously have been invested in securities, such as collateralized debt obligations, into other areas, including leveraged buyouts, known as LBOs.

"We're seeing fewer investments in subprime, but that money needs to be put to work so they're going into other credit markets," Larry Fink, the chief executive officer of investment firm BlackRock, said in an interview published by the *Financial Times* in April 2007. "Historically, when we've seen one problem, we've seen an adjustment throughout the marketplace. We've seen no indication of that yet. We've seen the actual opposite." Fear was absent and greed was in charge. The self-correcting mechanisms that typically limit money manager avarice were broken.

With more cash available to finance LBOs, private equity firms used ever-cheaper loans to buy companies. "There's capital everywhere," buyout doyen Henry Kravis of Kohlberg, Kravis, Roberts & Company said at an April conference in New York.

Measuring Liquidity

As a result, even some of the dealmakers who depended on cheap, no-strings-attached finance complained that money was too cheap. "The world isn't pricing risk appropriately," warned Steve Rattner, cofounder of buyout firm Quadrangle Group, at the beginning of 2007. "Investors are simply not being paid for the risks they're taking. Some of these deals will go bad." Philip Yea, chief executive officer of 3i Group, Europe's largest publicly traded venture capital and buyout firm, said in April 2007 that there was "too much liquidity in the system; there's too much debt available."

Dealmakers who depended on debt to make acquisitions were complaining of too much cheap credit. This was unheard of. The financiers who bought and sold companies for a living, though, were trapped on the same treadmill as their investing and trading colleagues. They didn't stop doing deals, even though a flood of liquidity inflated transaction prices to outrageous levels. They just held their noses, crossed their fingers, and paid higher prices. There was no glory—or bonus potential—in restraint, even for those who voiced their concerns that liquidity would drown the market.

Liquidity is notoriously hard to define or measure, but the Bank of England took a stab at quantifying global liquidity in its April 2007 Financial Stability Report. The central bank combined some key market measures: the gaps between buying and selling prices on bonds, currencies, and stocks; the ratio of market returns to trading volumes; and credit market spreads measuring how much investors charged to lend to companies rather than governments. The resulting index showed that financial market liquidity was at its highest level since at least 1992—as far back as the central bank's calculations went—and had doubled in the previous four years.

"Markets are currently very liquid and have been so over the past few years," the Bank of England wrote in the report. "Maximum debt levels for European LBOs are now consistently above seven or eight times earnings, whereas the maximum was around six times earnings a year ago." In other words, company buyers were loading more and more debt onto their acquisitions. That was fine when money was cheap and liquidity abundant, but potentially fatal should borrowing costs rise and refinancing become impossible, or if the economy faltered and companies couldn't make their interest payments.

With more money hunting in the same takeover pastures, deal prices rose and potential profits from buyout transactions shrank. In a low-yield environment, however, even a slowing bandwagon looked like an attractive investment vehicle to latecomers. "Inevitably, returns can't be as good as they've been," said David Rubenstein, a cofounder of the private equity firm Carlyle Group, in April 2007. "The returns that people will be able to get are better than anything else they can do with their money, at least that's legal."

Investment banks and hedge funds had found ways to take abundantly available money and multiply it many times over. Finding productive places for that leveraged cash to hang out, though, was getting harder and harder. That, combined with floods of liquidity from the Asian savings glut, produced waves of cash, each dollar or Euro looking for a profitable niche. Jeremy Grantham was right: there were bubbles everywhere, and those bubbles proved a prime driver behind the credit crisis.

By May 2007, the banking fraternity had engineered mergers and acquisitions worth more than $2 trillion for the year, a 60 percent increase on the value of transactions completed in the first five months of the previous year. For the M&A business, 2006 had been a record year, with $3.5 trillion of deals done. And 2007 was on track to trounce that total, which made at least one investment banking chief uneasy.

"We need a deal to go bad, as long as we're not in it," Bank of America chief executive officer Kenneth Lewis told the Swiss-American Chamber of Commerce in Zurich in May. "We are close to a time when we'll look back and say we did some stupid things. We need a little more sanity in a period when everyone feels invincible and thinks this is different." Sanity, though, remained in short supply.

FIVE

Judgment or Luck

The Profits Banks Couldn't Understand—or Protect

A crime has been committed. Yes, we insist, a crime. There is a victim (the helpless retiree, taxpayers funding losses, perhaps even capitalism and free society). There were plenty of bystanders. And there was a robber (overcompensated bankers who got fat bonuses hiding risks; overpaid quantitative risk managers selling patently bogus methods).
— Nassim Nicholas Taleb and Pablo Triana,
published on the Web Site of the
Financial Times on December 7, 2008

When an investment bank loses money on a trade, the aftermath resembles the crime scene of a particularly gruesome murder. Heads roll. The survivors analyze event details with forensic precision, scrutinize mistakes, tighten procedures, and (allegedly) learn lessons.

When an investment bank makes money on a trade, however, there is no corresponding attempt to understand the mechanics of the success. Participants slap backs and enjoy recalculated bonuses.

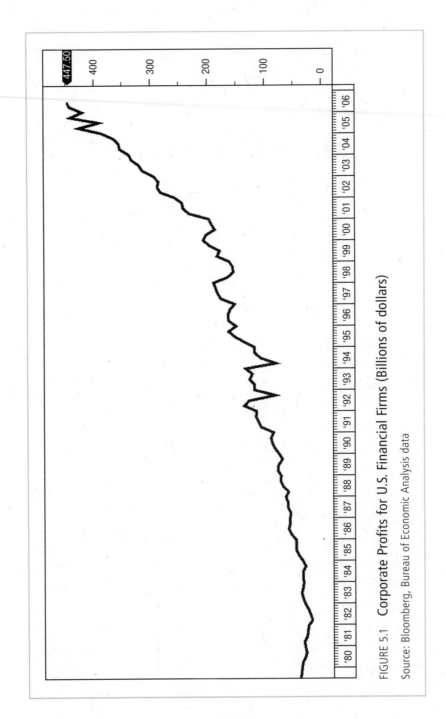

FIGURE 5.1 Corporate Profits for U.S. Financial Firms (Billions of dollars)

Source: Bloomberg, Bureau of Economic Analysis data

The trader tries to repeat the achievement and the manager attempts to take credit for nurturing such a phenomenal talent, but the bank makes no attempt to investigate whether the triumph was the result of sound judgment or sheer luck.

Profits rolled in at the height of the credit boom. Citigroup, for example, generated total net earnings of more than $90 billion between about March 2003 and November 2007. Banks congratulated themselves on their cleverness. They did not question whether their good fortune was mere happenstance or, as it turned out, the result of making bigger and bigger bets that were lucky rather than smart, in a near-perfect market environment created by providence, not proficiency. That somnambulism proved fatal. When the luck ran out, the lack of skill was laid bare.

Four U.K. academics specializing in psychology and behavioral science interviewed 118 London-based traders and managers from four unidentified investment banks, three with U.S. headquarters and one based in Europe, in a project designed to reveal the attributes of a good trader. The findings are in *Traders: Risks, Decisions and Management in Financial Markets*, published by Oxford University Press in 2004 and written by Mark Fenton-O'Creevy, senior lecturer in organizational behavior at the Open University Business School; Nigel Nicholson, professor of organizational behavior at London Business School; Emma Soane, senior lecturer at Kingston Business School; and Paul Willman, a professorial fellow of Balliol College, Oxford.

The quartet discovered that, though banks are willing to pay millions of dollars to their top profit makers, they have no idea how to spot or develop potential winners. Until a trader goes "ker-ching" or "ka-boom," the bank has no clue whether it has hired a star or a turkey. Even if the hiring turns out to be successful, banks make no attempt to work out the underlying reasons.

"The traders and managers we spoke to were almost all clear that superior performers had 'special' qualities, and yet no one was able to articulate clearly the precise set of skills and attributes implicated," the researchers wrote in their book. "There seem to be few resources directed toward identifying what makes a top trader, despite intense speculation on the subject, [and] the large costs of recruiting a new trader and giving them several years to see how potential develops into skill."

Traders put bank capital, and therefore equity, at risk every time they execute a transaction. Without understanding a trader's true skills, though, a bank can't evaluate the true risk it undertakes when it puts capital behind that employee's trades. Because cash seemed so freely available during the credit boom, banks paid zero attention to managing the traders who used bank capital to seed increasingly leveraged deals.

Inputs Versus Outputs

The professors were scathing about the lack of attention that the banks paid to running their trading teams. "Trader management is a training-free zone," they said. "In a combined 70 years of experience, the authors have never encountered so little management development in sophisticated organizations of vast resource. The combination of trader autonomy, reliance on bonus, and management spans of control generates an environment where managers see themselves as a safety net rather than as creators of value or profit," they wrote. "Put another way, trading environments rely too much on managing outputs."

Banks paid little attention to inputs, a blind spot common to financial institution managers and regulators during the credit boom. If market overseers had asked penetrating questions about how traders generated fantastic profits, they surely would have realized that the financial system was mushrooming into an enormous inverted pyramid, with a tiny triangle of real money at the base trying to buttress towering layers of debt and derivatives. But banks and regulators had little incentive to ask probing questions. Banks were getting rich. Regulators, for their part, held to a blind faith that banks must be doing something right to amass such riches. So long as they kept at it, profits would continue to accumulate.

The academic researchers used a variety of tests to assess trading prowess. One featured a chart on a computer screen. The line on the graph started at zero, and then rose or fell every half second for 50 seconds. Researchers told traders that pressing keyboard keys Z, X, or C might affect how the chart developed.

When the chart stopped moving, researchers asked traders how much influence their typing had. In fact the typing, no matter how frenetic, had no effect on graph development. Some traders realized that the chart's progress was predetermined, but others were convinced that they had full control of the line's movements. A roomful of shirt-sleeved guys (only two of the 118 analysis participants were female) bashing impotently at a set of computer keyboards seems in some ways an ideal image to summarize the origins of the credit crunch.

Because banks don't spend enough time investigating where and how they make money, they don't know when—or how—they should change in varying market climates. Investors, too, are in the dark. Because bank earnings reports are masterworks in opacity, even the most conscientious investor would struggle to accurately dissect the interaction between profitability and probability. "A banking specialist PhD who has spent twenty years at Bank College studying nothing but banks, and whose every waking second is committed to understanding banks, would struggle to conduct due diligence upon banks consistent with making an informed assessment of the risks they hold and the risk they represent," says Tim Price, director of investments at PFP Wealth Management in London.

Investment banks generated much of their credit boom profits by using the derivatives market to bend and shape the price of money. The new breeds of complicated derivatives, however, hadn't been through sufficiently severe crises for traders to understand how these investments might behave under pressure.

Once again, the lessons of history should have made the banking community slow to trust untested investment strategies. In the run up to the 1987 stock market crash, banks automated trading decisions for program trades and portfolio insurance, using computer programs that could exploit price discrepancies faster than a human trader could. The computer programs could also follow predetermined selling levels to protect against losses. Individually, the new techniques worked well. Collectively, they proved disastrous, as they prompted everyone to run simultaneously for the same exit at the first sign of trouble.

"The simultaneous operation of the trading prescription of these methods caused a price decline across major stock markets," according to *The New Palgrave Dictionary of Money & Finance*, published in 1992 in three volumes by The Macmillan Press. "The crash of 1987 came as a surprise test of the system. Just as a formerly promising piece of technology that unexpectedly fails a stress test loses value, so does a widespread financial innovation."

Compliant Compliance

A decade after that crash, banks risked billions of dollars on trading ideas that relied on mathematical models, used scant historical data to assess their vulnerability to market shocks, and didn't consider how those trades would perform if future price behavior turned out to be different than it had been in the very recent past. During the credit boom, however, even the gamekeepers—who were supposed to restrain trader excess—lost their collective nerve.

In August 2008, *The Economist* published an article by an anonymous risk manager at what the weekly magazine called a "large global bank." The author described the insiders responsible for protecting banks from themselves, delivering a damning indictment of the ways they dishonorably discharged their duties. The employees who should have kept investment bank sewers from backing up were asleep at the stopcocks, actively discouraged from ringing any alarm bells, and easily cowed by the hostility that met any attempts they did make to curb risky behavior.

"Often in meetings, our gut reactions as risk managers were negative," the risk manager wrote. "But it was difficult to come up with hard and fast arguments for why you should decline a transaction, especially when you were sitting opposite a team that had worked for weeks on a proposal, which you had received an hour before the meeting started." How on God's green earth could even the most experienced credit officer judge the merits of a complex transaction in just sixty minutes? Clearly, the risk department should have demanded more time to decide whether the sixteen beans of profit the traders claimed were really generated by multiplying two beans of revenue by eight beans of risk.

Basic mathematical skills were also missing in action. "We had not paid enough attention to the ever-growing mountain of highly rated but potentially illiquid assets," the article says. "We had not fully appreciated that 20 percent of a very large number can inflict far greater losses than 80 percent of a small number." Letting traders build piles of complicated, insufficiently scrutinized debt is a recipe for creating an opaque, unfathomable, and downright dangerous bank balance sheet—exactly what happened.

"Most of the time the business line would simply not take no for an answer, especially if the profits were big enough," the author writes. "This made it hard to discourage transactions. If a risk manager said no, he was immediately on a collision course with the business line. The risk thinking therefore leaned toward giving the benefit of the doubt to the risk-takers." A risk department that only says yes has little purpose, apart from creating the pretense of prudence that regulators may demand.

Banks often benefited from having quiet compliance departments, or so it seems. Société Générale blamed Jérôme Kerviel, a back room clerk who rose to become a junior trader, for accumulating trading losses that reached an astronomical €4.9 billion before the firm discovered the losses in 2008. Kerviel admitted lying, faking trading authorizations, and using other people's passwords to log into the bank's computer system. He asserts, however, that his superiors at the bank's Paris headquarters knew what he was up to and turned a blind eye while he exceeded trading limits and made uninsured bets—as long, that is, as he was making money.

Kerviel's accusation sounds less outrageous when we consider banking's increasingly docile internal watchdogs. Compliance officers, as risk managers are also known, are paid to ensure that a bank's traders comply with internal regulations and external directives. In the credit boom, they became compliant officers instead. Traders made money on questionable transactions, it's true, but so did compliance officers. Their incomes depended on allowing deals to happen.

Any compliance officer who said "no" to even the most foolhardy proposal shrank the firm's total bonus pool and ran the risk of being overruled, ostracized, or even fired. Paul Moore was head of risk at the U.K. institution HBOS—formed from a merger between Halifax and Bank of Scotland—from 2002 to 2005, when it was Britain's biggest mortgage company. He alleges that he lost his job for telling his bosses that the bank was jeopardizing its own safety by selling products to clients that the customers didn't understand, and that regulators failed to investigate his accusations. Both the authorities and his former employer deny the charges.

Alpha and Beta

In the financial markets, alpha and beta aren't just Greek letters. Beta refers to profits made just by being in the market. Owning the thirty stocks in the Dow Jones Industrial Average in the same proportion as they appear in the index, for example, means that investment value will increase or decrease in direct proportion to index performance. Alpha is the extra return you make by being clever—scaling back your investment in Caterpillar, say, to boost your Boeing holdings, because you expect the aircraft maker to do better than the construction industry. You'll beat the index if your analysis is correct. The credit boom created the illusion that money managers everywhere were earning tons of alpha.

Hedge funds love the idea of alpha because it justifies their payment structure by allowing them to claim that they provide added investment strategy value. Detractors say that hedge funds levy outsized fees on the pretext of generating lots of clever alpha, when they are really just seizing the beta available to anyone. Indeed, the $1.4 trillion hedge fund industry has only a handful of firms who can consistently beat their benchmarks year in and year out, which suggests that the critics have a point. "Fees in hedge funds are ridiculous, period," Harry Kat, professor of risk management, at London's Cass Business School, told a hedge fund conference in February 2007. "I'm not saying these managers don't have any skill; they just don't have enough to justify their fees."

Black Swans and Unknown Unknowns

Hedge fund manager Nassim Nicholas Taleb is one of the most vocal skeptics about the ability of traders and money managers to make money consistently. Taleb's 2001 book, *Fooled by Randomness*, as well as an April 2002 profile written by Malcolm Gladwell in *The New Yorker*, outline Taleb's theory that luck plays a huge, unacknowledged role in successful trades. In April 2007, Taleb published a second book, *The Black Swan: The Impact of the Highly Improbable*, which became an instant bestseller.

Taleb writes that the human race is dangerously blind to the possibility of unlikely events and reluctant to accept their unpredictability when they do occur. All swans were believed to be white, until black swans were discovered in Australia. A black swan, in Taleb's argument, is an incredibly improbable event with a colossal impact: the terrorist attacks of September 11, 2001, or the rise of Google. Human beings typically rationalize such events, making them appear more predictable than they are and leaving us equally unprepared to deal with the next unforeseeable event.

A farmer can feed a turkey for a thousand days but wring the bird's neck on day 1,001. "A thousand days cannot prove you right, but one day can prove you to be wrong," Taleb writes. The same inductive fallacy that proves fatal for the turkey—expecting the future to be just like the past—left the credit-rating companies blind to the dangers posed by the derivatives to which they blithely assigned top grades, left banks relying on mathematical trading models that can't compute nonlinear outcome probability, and infected the computer models that the banking community relied on to stress test investments. By 2007, the finance industry was acting as if both known unknowns and unknown unknowns were consigned to history.

Taleb didn't predict the credit crunch, but that's not his point. Taleb argues that one-time, big-impact events such as the global credit crunch are intrinsically unpredictable. That doesn't mean, however, that we can act as if such occurrences will never happen. If anything, the larger-scale damage that unforeseen events can inflict, compared to the lesser losses created by more mundane threats, should encourage us to defend ourselves against chance events.

Taleb did, however, suggest that the financial industry could suffer greatly from a negative, chance event. The globalized economy gives "the appearance of stability" even as it "creates devastating black swans," Taleb writes. "We have never before lived under the threat of a global collapse. The financial ecology is swelling into gigantic, incestuous, bureaucratic banks—when one falls, they all fall."

Belatedly, regulators began to realize that computer models that scrutinize financial firms' discrete, individual risks say very little about the real likelihood of a one-off disaster. They say absolutely nothing about the odds of a generalized failure, nor can they predict the possible results of a system-wide malfunction.

"Banks often model the effect of even severe macroeconomic shocks as if they were occurring to the bank in isolation," Nigel Jenkinson, the executive director for financial stability at the Bank of England, told a July 2007 conference organized by the European Central Bank in Frankfurt. "An important implication is that many firm-level stress tests may consequently underestimate the possible impact of adverse shocks. If a shock is sufficiently large, the financial network may consequently act as a conduit for transmitting rather than absorbing risk. The flip side of greater integration is that it may have lowered the frequency but increased the magnitude of potential financial crises."

The Beginning of a "Savage Bear Market"

By the first half of 2007, money was almost free and financial markets remained oblivious to the danger of an imminent crisis. Investors charged an average of just 96 basis points more to lend money to U.S. companies in the corporate bond market than they demanded from the U.S. government, according to indexes compiled by Credit Suisse Group. That spread had been as high as 246 basis points in October 2002 and had a five-year average of 111 basis points. Even the riskiest borrowers paid a yield premium to government debt of just 300 basis points, compared with a twenty-year average of more than 550 basis points.

Just as some sharks have to keep moving to stay alive, so money managers had to continue investing to stay in business, however overpriced financial assets became. With too much money chasing too few deals, portfolio managers felt that they couldn't afford the luxury of shunning any borrowers, no matter how tarnished their histories. At the beginning of the decade, for example, a company called Thai Petrochemical Industry PCL had defaulted on its bonds and been declared insolvent, with debts of $3.5 billion, in what was then Thailand's biggest bankruptcy. By May 2007, the company had rebranded itself as IRPC PCL, grown to become the nation's biggest petrochemicals maker, and persuaded international investors to lend it $400 million by buying the company's new bonds.

As the returns available on real assets such as bonds waned, more and more investors turned to the bigger bets available in derivatives' virtual world. "Our derivatives business is continuing to grow very strongly," Huw Jenkins, head of investment banking at Swiss bank UBS AG, said in May 2007. "In fact, we are now achieving the same amount of revenues out of our derivatives business as we are achieving out of our cash business, all from a much lower cost base."

It is much cheaper for an investment bank to ask a couple of traders to sit with a spreadsheet and create new products out of thin air than it is to send a team on the road to persuade an institution to sell new bonds, convince a company to list its shares on a stock exchange, or encourage two competitors to merge. Derivatives, though, get their name for a reason: they derive their value from some other asset. It's worrying that one of the biggest banks in the world was making more profit from its derivatives business than from the underlying markets, especially because the derivatives field was precisely where flawed computer models held the most sway. As corporate bond prices raced ever higher, some strategists reached for their furry bear suits.

"We are growing extremely negative on credit markets, which we see as in a bubble," Tim Bond, head of asset allocation at Barclays Capital in London, wrote in a May 2007 research note. "U.S. companies are re-leveraging aggressively in an attempt to substitute earnings per share growth for earnings growth. 2008 should see a fairly savage bear market for credit, a large rise in defaults and an end to easy liquidity conditions." Even "savage" would ultimately be inadequate to describe the credit boom's demise.

SIX

Knight in Rusty Armor

An Ill-Advised Rescue Helps Show Banks Just How Much
Value Their Collateralized Debt Has Lost

*A man is not independent, and cannot afford views' which might
interfere with his bread and butter. If he would prosper, he must train
with the majority; in matters of large moment, like politics and reli-
gion, he must think and feel with the bulk of his neighbors, or suffer
damage in his social standing and in his business prosperities. He
must get his opinions from other people; he must reason out none for
himself; he must have no first-hand views.*
— MARK TWAIN, CORN-PONE OPINIONS, 1905

THE BUSINESS OF BANKING depends on trust. For the industry's business
model to succeed, depositors must have faith that the money in their
checking accounts will be available instantaneously and on demand.

Even in the age of electronic commerce, many customers may
subconsciously picture bank accounts as vaults containing piles of
neatly stacked banknotes, with a nametag and account number
affixed to each bundle.

The truth, of course, is very different. Your money isn't sitting
patiently in the bank's basement, waiting to race upstairs to the ATM

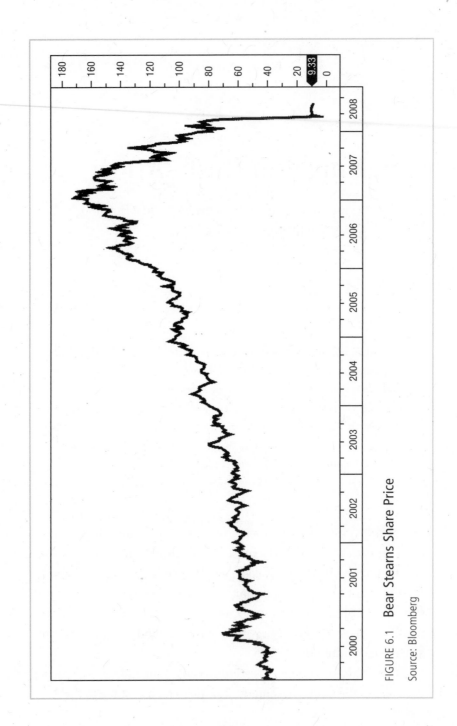

FIGURE 6.1 Bear Stearns Share Price

Source: Bloomberg

when you make a withdrawal. Your cash is having the time of its life in the global financial casino, drunk on leverage and high on liquidity. Bank deposits, as ever, helped small businesses grow and oiled the commercial wheels of local communities. Deposits have also become seed capital for exotic financial adventures, funding wind farms in Scotland, artificial islands in Asia, and skyscrapers in the Middle East. (The Glass-Steagall Act, introduced in the 1930s to separate retail banking from investment banking in the United States tried to prevent depositors' funds from taking wild rides. President Bill Clinton's administration repealed that law in 1999.)

As part of this business model, a bank also must trust that only a handful of its customers will want their money at any one time. By taking deposits, the bank is effectively borrowing from its depositors, who can demand loan repayment at any time. It then uses those deposits to make longer-term investments. In technical terms, it is borrowing short to lend long—a risky strategy if your money fails to return from its voyages in time for you to reclaim it.

That trust-based system doesn't just operate between banks and their customers. It also plays an essential role helping banks trade with each other. (Banks routinely borrow from one another to satisfy regulatory requirements or cash demand.) Should that trust evaporate, justifiably or not, an institution can rapidly become the redheaded stepchild of the financial markets, starved of the uninterrupted flow of liquidity it needs to remain viable. The credit crunch revealed that trust between members of the financial community is all but nonexistent during times of stress. Bankers are, at heart, cannibals.

Bear Stearns Funds Go Bang

A dispute erupted in the middle of 2007 between Bear Stearns, which at the time was the biggest hedge fund broker, and its fellow investment banks. By then, Wall Street firms should have been fully aware of the noxious fumes seeping out of the subprime shambles. They should have been drawing up plans to circle the wagons and investigating ways to close ranks, defending against the brewing financial storm. Instead, they turned on each other, making the credit crunch infinitely worse than it might otherwise have been.

The altercation between Bear Stearns and its peers encapsulated many of the dilemmas that were beginning to bubble to the surface of the subprime quagmire, dilemmas that would become persistent features of the credit crunch. How much money had investors gambled? How much of it, if any, was real money? What were the true values of the investments on which Wall Street had gambled? Could Wall Street realistically predict the financial impact of a worst-case scenario? Had risk been sliced and diced and dispersed, or multiplied and refocused?

As with many disputes, this fight's origins took place long before open war broke out. Bear Stearns raised almost $2 billion from clients to create two investment funds: the Bear Stearns High-Grade Structured Credit Strategies Fund, which began operating in October 2003, and the Bear Stearns High-Grade Structured Credit Strategies Enhanced Leverage Fund, which started in August 2006. Note the subtle difference between the two names. The latter fund offered "enhanced leverage," which meant borrowing about twenty times as much money as clients put in, so that it could make bigger bets.

The funds, run by trader Ralph Cioffi, specialized in buying collateralized-debt obligations and started to struggle as the price of mortgage-backed bonds began to slip. In both respects, they were similar to a thousand other ventures, many of which also found themselves in trouble as the U.S. subprime mortgage market imploded, sending shocks through the CDO market and out into the wider worlds of finance and economics.

Banks' Ill-Advised Loans

The Bear Stearns funds didn't just gather equity from individual investors, however. In the prevailing go-go, can't fail, anything goes zeitgeist, banks lent the funds money, allowing the funds to make total bets that were twenty or even thirty times greater than the funds' stake money. They erected an edifice of borrowed money on a slender cash base, reasoning that staking $200 million is twenty times more lucrative than pledging $10 million—as long as the gamble pays off.

Banks, for their part, didn't worry about these bets. They thought they could seize the hedge funds' assets if the deals went awry.

The fund structures were reminiscent of the financial strategies used by subprime mortgage lenders such as New Century, which used loans to keep the business afloat for as long as possible, borrowing short-term cash to make long-term gambles. The structures were equally vulnerable to collapse as the credit crunch worsened.

As we know now, of course, the gamble did go awry. CDO values crumbled, and banks demanded more security against the loans, a move known as a collateral or margin call. In that situation, the borrower must typically raise cash by selling assets, which further depresses fund value and often leads to a death spiral.

"There have been some counterparties who have moved to liquidate collateral," Bear Stearns chief financial officer Samuel Molinaro said on a June 22 conference call. "When you have difficulty raising liquidity to meet margin calls, more margin calls come and it becomes a bit of a vicious circle." In the first four months of 2007, the so-called enhanced fund had lost more than 20 percent of its value. In June, Bear Stearns told investors they could not withdraw their cash from the fund.

As the credit crunch overwhelmed more and more investment funds, many managers barred withdrawals. It was a last resort, designed to avoid a fire sale of fund assets to satisfy redemption demands, but it had a disastrous side effect. It made investors think twice, even about funds that were doing comparatively well, and start considering a reduction in their risk exposures.

Most funds have a lockup period, which requires investors to leave cash in for a preset length of time. The policy gives fund managers scope to pursue investment strategies over sufficiently long time horizons. Telling investors they can't withdraw their current account values even when a lockup period has expired, however, is tantamount to an bank refusing to hand over the balance of your savings account because it's less than it was last month. By making this move, investment banks helped to eliminate customer trust.

The decision was also part of managers' refusal to face the uncomfortable truth. CDO values were not likely to recover, so locking a fund just delayed the inevitable. At some point, the funds would have to sell assets at whatever price was available, however low, and investors would have to swallow their losses.

By the time Bear Stearns locked the fund doors, some of the market's most damaged CDOs fetched prices 70 percent below their original valuations. When traders know that an investor must sell assets to raise cash, they move in for the kill, offering rock-bottom prices in the hope of snapping up a bargain. The less each asset is worth, the more the fund must sell to fulfill lender demands—and so the spiral deepens.

As Bear Stearns fought to keep the two funds breathing, it asked its peers for help in mounting a rescue attempt. The answer was a resounding "no" from firms including Cantor Fitzgerald, JPMorgan Chase & Company and Lehman Brothers Holdings, who had traded with and lent to the funds. Revenge may well have played a part in motivating those refusals. Nine years earlier, Bear Stearns had refused to participate in the bailout of Long-Term Capital Management; the Federal Reserve cajoled other Wall Street firms into paying for that rescue.

Mark to Market—and to Panic

Merrill Lynch promptly seized $850 million of bonds that the Bear Stearns funds had pledged as loan collateral. Along with other firms that had also reclaimed collateral, Merrill began trying to offload these securities. Though Merrill was entitled to pursue this course of action, a stronger sense of collective responsibility, and a closer look at its decision's wider implications, might have prompted it to delay the sale.

The prospect of an auction of price-damaged CDOs triggered a ripple of panic throughout the investment community. By the middle of 2007, CDO valuations were operating on a strict "don't ask, don't tell" basis: don't ask me what price your CDO could bring, and I won't tell anyone what I think its current value might be.

CDOs were like landmines waiting to detonate in the banking industry's balance sheets, the register of a company's assets and liabilities. By law at the time, securities firms and their regulators valued assets on a mark-to-market basis: assets were worth whatever selling price they might bring in the current market. Even companies with no interest in selling an investment still had to assign it a balance sheet value, with too-low totals carrying potential regulatory consequences.

The quickest way to value an asset is to research the recent selling price of another, very similar asset. (Real estate agents do this to determine a home's proper listing price.) If you own an apple and someone sells another apple at a particular price, your apple is likely worth the same price.

Merrill Lynch's threatened sale of sequestered assets was dangerous because it jeopardized the sham that apples—or CDOs, in this case—were still worth a sum close to what investors had paid for them. If the price has fallen since you bought your apple, under mark-to-market accounting you must write down its value to the new, lower level. Your asset-to-liabilities ratio deteriorates, perhaps badly enough that your liabilities exceed your assets and you become insolvent. If no one sells an apple, however, you may get away with pretending that your apple's value hasn't changed—even if you suspect it is rotten to the core.

The latter approach became known as "marking-to-myth," and it helps explain the credit crunch's iceberg-like progress. Only the jagged, hostile surface was visible at first, showing up in the U.S. subprime market. The calamity's true proportions took many months to emerge from below the financial waves.

Even as CDO values deteriorated, banks used every trick in the accounting book to delay admitting the true worth of these securities. Some banks tried moving assets from the trading book to the banking book, a kind of pledge that a bank will never sell the rotten apple and so it is still worth its full initial value. Other investors reclassified securities as Level 3 assets, a claim that an investment is so complex and trades so infrequently that any attempt to pin down a current price is futile. Eventually, though, so many assets deteriorated so badly that banks ran out of ways to shift them from column to column on the balance sheet. More and more banks had to acknowledge their losses.

Not everyone agrees that the mark-to-market accounting rule is a good one. "I spent my whole life at Goldman Sachs believing in mark-to-market accounting," Robert Rubin, who spent 26 years at the firm and was cochairman in the early 1990s, told a New York meeting on January 27, 2009. "Having said that, if you look at the experience from the last two years, I think mark-to-market accounting has led to terrible vicious cycles in asset prices." Supporters of marking to market argue that it is the only way to guarantee transparency and force banks to truthfully disclose any problems lurking in their balance sheets.

Opponents say the rule obliges banks to prematurely write off assets that might have suffered a temporary decline in value and doesn't give sufficient breathing space for recovery over the long run. As the economist John Maynard Keynes said, though, in the long run we are all dead. Rubin, who went on to be U.S. Treasury secretary and then spent ten years at Citigroup before retiring from his position there as senior counselor in January 2009, said he favored a system known as reserve accounting, under which assets such as loans are carried on the balance sheet at what they originally cost, with cash set aside to offset any losses that might arise. It is very hard to argue that less transparency—which is what mark-to-market alternatives all offer, in on way or another—is desirable.

On April 2, 2009, the Financial Accounting Standards Board (FASB) eased mark-to-market rules. The new regulations still require financial institutions to mark assets at market prices, but more so in a steady market and less so in an inactive market. The rule change, however, came too late for the two Bear Stearns funds.

Ratings Cuts

The credit-rating companies belatedly acknowledged their wildly over-optimistic initial analyses of CDO values. The Bank for International Settlements calculates that Moody's cut its assessment of $5 billion in bonds backed by subprime mortgages and started reviewing a further 184 pieces of mortgage-backed CDOs, all during just three days in July 2007. Standard & Poor's, meanwhile, said it was likely to downgrade $7.3 billion of mortgage-backed bonds created in the previous year. Thousands of Americans couldn't meet their mortgage obligations, with disastrous consequences for the bonds built on atop their loans.

The financial industry, though, still denied the implications of failing subprime mortgages. On June 14, 2007, Lehman Brothers chief financial officer Chris O'Meara said any dangers arising from missed mortgage payments were "well contained" and would not "create a big event in the economy." Twelve days later, Freddie Mac treasurer Timothy Bitsberger called the problems among subprime borrowers "severe but contained." And the following day, Merrill

Lynch chief executive officer Stanley O'Neal called the mortgage market problem "reasonably well contained," and said there were "no clear signs it's spilling over into other subsets of the bond market, the fixed-income market and the credit market."

O'Neal's own chief investment strategist was far less relaxed. "The financial liquidity spigot is starting to tighten," Merrill's Richard Bernstein warned in a July research note. "The childhood alliteration to remember how to turn a spigot is 'righty-tighty, lefty-loosey.' It's now righty-tighty time for the financial markets." Later that month, Citigroup chief executive officer Charles Prince told the *Financial Times* that "as long as the music is playing, you've got to get up and dance."

Even with the dancehall collapsing around their ears, Wall Street's executives refused to admit that the music was about to stop. They were like forced contestants in a dance marathon; if they tried to rest, they'd be expelled. No one wanted to be the first to retire from the competition. The pretense of confidence had to be maintained.

A Different Food Chain

Bear Stearns ultimately tried to bail out the failing funds at its own expense, a face-saving exercise that cost about $3 billion and didn't even work. This was an astonishing turn of events, with far-reaching implications for how the credit crunch would play out.

Wall Street firms hadn't just engineered the creation of the derivatives market and lent most of the money that financed CDO purchases. Now they might also find themselves the reluctant owners of billions of dollars of those CDOs in a souring market. Bear Stearns wasn't obliged to take financial responsibility for its two funds' failure. Its executives thought absorbing those losses was a price worth paying to avoid collateral damage to the firm's reputation.

Bear Stearns' self-financed fund bailout created a new set of risks for the banking community. Blaine Frantz, a credit analyst at

Moody's, wrote in a June 22 report that the issue of "moral responsibility" was a wild card for Wall Street because "it raises important questions around potential reputation risk."

Other firms were also facing similar disasters in hedge funds bearing their names. These companies might also feel subjectively motivated to spend money to salvage affiliates, but there was no way of knowing to whom that could happen or how much it might cost. Ratings companies couldn't incorporate that risk into the spreadsheets used to assess company's creditworthiness, adding yet another element of uncertainty to the market outlook.

The derivatives market food chain looked a little different and a lot more dangerous. How much of the toxic product was really in the hands of end investors? How much was just a click of an accountant's calculator away from flooding back onto the banks themselves?

In July 2007, Bear Stearns filed for bankruptcy protection for the two damaged funds. In June 2008, the Federal Bureau of Investigation arrested Ralph Cioffi and his colleague Matthew Tannin on allegations of securities fraud, after investigating whether they had misled fund investors. The two were the first Wall Street executives to face criminal charges as a result of the subprime mortgage market's collapse.

That same month, the United Kingdom Barclays Bank filed a lawsuit alleging that Bear Stearns' fund managers had concealed just how badly their investments were doing. The legal action, which Barclays dropped in February 2009, revealed that Barclays had been the sole investor in the enhanced fund, and had lost "almost all" of a $400 million investment it made after August 2006.

The death of the Bear Stearns funds had global ramifications, too. An Asian insurance company, Taiwan Life Insurance Company, took a $13 million loss for the first half of 2007 because it had invested money with one of the failed funds. In France, stockbroker and money manager Oddo & Cie said it was closing three funds overseeing a total of €1 billion because of what it called the "unprecedented" crisis in U.S. asset-backed bonds—even though half the CDOs the funds had bought were near the very top of the credit-rating scale, with grades of AAA or AA. And by the end of August, German bank IKB Deutsche Industriebank was in enough trouble to need a €3.5 billion government rescue, as the aftershocks rumbled through the markets, destroying the value of previously intact securities and leaving more and more banks holding impaired assets.

This tectonic shift in financial geography went unpunished at the time. Even as it became clear that publicity-conscious banks might ride to the rescue of funds they sponsored but for which they were not liable, the ratings companies and the regulatory authorities continued to underestimate the danger. "The subprime exposures of the major U.S. investment banks and institutionally active commercial banks do not have negative rating implications at this time," Moody's said in a myopic August 3 report.

In August 2007, Goldman Sachs elected to spend $2 billion bolstering its tottering Global Equity Opportunities Fund, which had lost about 28 percent of its value in a month. Goldman contended that "current values that the market is assigning to the assets underlying various funds represent a discount that is not supported by the fundamentals." Standard & Poor's analysts Scott Sprinzen and Diane Hinton responded with a research note that said "we are concerned that this action on the part of Goldman is also being taken to protect Goldman Sachs Asset Management's image in the market, pointing up moral hazard risks related to GSAM that go beyond what we had assumed in our analysis."

Guessing at Write-Downs

Even when regulators and investors finally estimated the total possible write-offs, those guesses proved woefully inadequate. Around July

2007, Switzerland's Credit Suisse Group predicted that the world's financial firms faced write-downs worth a total of $52 billion. Pacific Investment Management Company, which manages the world's biggest bond fund, reckoned $75 billion might disappear. Germany's Deutsche Bank was a bit more pessimistic, putting the value destruction at $90 billion.

Those numbers proved to be a little low. Global write-downs among financial firms passed the $1 trillion mark by the end of 2008. In January 2009, the International Monetary Fund predicted that the total would eventually reach $2.2 trillion. In eighteen months the markets saw that even their gloomiest prognosis was wrong by a factor of 10.

Around the world, the banks themselves were struggling to work out how much trouble was hiding in the depths of their balance sheets. For example, DBS Group Holdings Ltd., Singapore's biggest bank, said on August 7 that it had searched through its accounting closets and calculated that it had 1.4 billion Singapore dollars, the equivalent of about $921 million at the time, at stake in collateralized-debt obligations. Less than a month later, it revised that figure to S$2.4 billion. In its initial audit, the bank overlooked its apparently substantial commitment to its Red Orchid Secured Assets unit.

Regulators snoozed through the credit boom, believing that the market was slicing, dicing, and dispersing risk. Instead, the world of finance was incestuous, interconnected, and horribly vulnerable to any hiccups in its supply of easy money.

SEVEN

The Noose Tightens

Frozen Money Markets Confound Central Bankers,
Hurt Consumers, and Drive Imploding Investments Back
onto Bankers' Books

*The rulers of the exchange of mankind's goods have failed. There must
be an end to a conduct in banking and in business which too often has
given to a sacred trust the likeness of callous and selfish wrongdoing.*

—U.S. PRESIDENT FRANKLIN D. ROOSEVELT,
IN HIS 1933 INAUGURATION ADDRESS

DROP A FROG into a pan of boiling water, and the frog will desperately try
to jump out. Slip the frog into a pan of lukewarm water, however, and
bring the water to its boiling point over the course of several minutes,
and the frog will allegedly surrender to its fate. On August 9, 2007,
the global financial market suddenly realized, like that frog, that it was
trapped in hot water with no prospect of escape.

There is no single, credible reason why an otherwise unremark-
able Thursday turned into a kind of Judgment Day on the financial
world's excesses.

As trading began in Europe, the French bank BNP Paribas told
investors that it was freezing redemptions from three investment funds

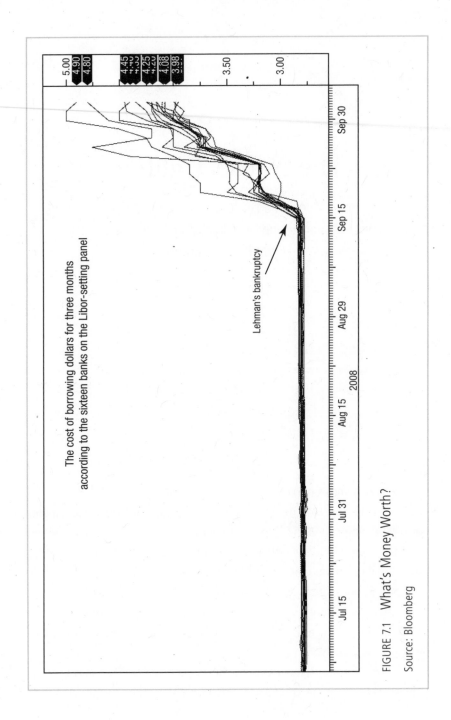

The cost of borrowing dollars for three months according to the sixteen banks on the Libor-setting panel

Lehman's bankruptcy

5.00
4.90
4.80

4.45
4.~~

4.25
4.~~
4.08
3.98
3.~~

3.50

3.00

Jul 15   Jul 31   Aug 15   Aug 29   Sep 15   Sep 30

2008

FIGURE 7.1   What's Money Worth?

Source: Bloomberg

that it controlled. By then, this was an almost common occurrence. Bear Stearns had frozen redemptions from its two failing funds more than a month earlier, and barred withdrawals from a third fund on August 1. An Australian hedge fund, Absolute Capital Group, locked investors in on July 26, and German fund manager Union Investments barred further withdrawals from one of its funds on August 3, after investors pulled out about 10 percent of their money. Investors in the BNP Paribas funds may have been dismayed when the bank blocked withdrawals, but they probably weren't astonished.

Libor Freezes Over

As the morning progressed, though, rumors began to circulate, saying that global banks operating in London were refusing to lend to each other. If that was true, it was unprecedented.

Money is the lifeblood of financial markets. Much of it flows through something called the interbank market, also known as the money market. Each day, banks use the money market to lend and borrow billions of dollars. Any institution—from an insurance company to a manufacturer—can make the most of surplus cash by entrusting it to the interbank market, where it earns interest until the institution needs it again. Much of this recycling takes place in the London money market, which helps money stream from those who have a surplus to those who have a need—and can pay to fill it.

How much should it cost to borrow money on the London money market? An organization called the British Bankers' Association sets that rate every day at about 11:00 a.m., after asking a panel of bankers what interest rates they each think their banks would pay to borrow a variety of currencies for a set of different time periods. Collectively, that suite of rates is known as Libor, which stands for the London Interbank Offered Rates.

At the time the credit crunch was taking off, sixteen banks set the most important Libor levels, which are the three-month interest rates for U.S. dollars and British pounds. (The European Banking Federation sets the comparable rate for euros in a similar fashion on the Continent.) Those three-month interest rates have global significance: the Bank for International Settlements, which is kind of a central bank for central banks, estimates that an amazing $360 trillion of financial securities are tied in one way or another to Libor. Your credit card interest rate is effectively set in London, as are house payments on a floating-rate mortgage or car payments on a loan made without a fixed interest rate. Companies that use bank loans to upgrade equipment or build a new factory pay an interest rate that's based on Libor.

Fundamentally, bankers must know how much money should cost at any given time—as a banknote, a share of a company, or a debt instrument such as a bond. Just as a farmer with no idea how much to charge for his apples will soon go broke, a banker unable to gauge the proper interest rate on a three-month loan will struggle to make sense of the rest of the financial world.

On August 9, London's money market bankers realized that the financial environment was shaky—so shaky that they couldn't estimate the proper price of money. They didn't know how many toxic assets their own banks would ultimately have to bring back onto their balance sheets, so they didn't know how much cash they would need to plug the newly evident holes created by these toxic assets.

Banks certainly couldn't assess how badly damaged their industry neighbors would likely become. As the credit-rating company Moody's had said in a report published the previous week, the lack of "public disclosures and position transparency make it virtually impossible for investors to accurately quantify each firm's credit, market and liquidity exposures within the troubled sector." No one, including the banks themselves, was in any position to judge how deeply banks' toxic assets would wound the solvency of the global financial system. Would money be only moderately more valuable than usual, or more valuable than life itself? No one knew.

The bankers decided it was safer to keep their cash than to lend it to others in the money market, so they tried to push the cost of cash high enough to deter anyone from borrowing. When the daily Libor settings were published that Thursday morning, it was clear that the money markets were starting to freeze. No one, it seemed, was ready to lend.

As the British Bankers Association transmitted the new interest rates it had collected from the London banking community, it became clear that the credit crunch was about to squeeze the real economy. The rate that banks charge each other to borrow dollars overnight leaped to its highest level since the beginning of 2001, soaring to 5.86 percent from 5.35 percent. Some banks, including Bank of America and Barclays, said they were seeing overnight dollar rates of 6 percent at a time when the Fed was trying to steer borrowing costs at 5.25 percent. The economic outlook was changing.

Overnight euro borrowing rates jumped 0.2 percent to 4.31 percent. With credit suddenly in short supply, the European Central Bank attempted to offset that increase by offering unlimited cash to the region's banks. Banks accepted an unprecedented $130 billion, even more than they borrowed to shore up the financial system in the wake of the September 11, 2001, terror attacks. Deposit rates went wild. In the space of just five hours, the interest rates available in a euro-denominated account fluctuated between 4 percent and 4.62 percent, as traders tried and failed to gauge the value of money.

August 9 marked the beginning of the credit crunch proper. From the moment banks became reluctant to lend to each other, it was clear that their willingness to provide funds to consumers and companies would also quickly evaporate. The best brains in banking had used virtual money and leverage to invent exotic financial devices. Now they understood that their creations were toxic, and that the contagion threatened to wreck a basic building block in banking's structure: institutions' willingness to lend each other money.

Trust Unravels

In a single day, the likely consequences of earlier reckless lending and investing became apparent. The system of trust that underpins the global web of financial contracts began to unravel. Banks began a "dash for cash," hoarding capital instead of distributing it. "Unable to access the market or dispose of securities in an orderly fashion, banks and institutions are raising their desired holdings of cash," noted Nick Parsons, head of markets strategy at National Australia Bank's London office.

The financial community's fears had another, self-fulfilling consequence. If the banks didn't trust each other, why should anyone trust the banks? If they were so concerned about each other's mounting liabilities, why would investors want to own their shares? And if they wouldn't lend to each other, why should other institutions make their own excess funds available to the money markets? Both bank stock and bank bond debt were immediately less desirable, and institutions all over the world sat on their cash rather than send it to the money markets.

Money instantly became more expensive. The cost of borrowing dollars jumped overnight by more than half a percentage point to 5.86 percent, its highest level in more than six years. It was a huge leap, given that the Federal Reserve's target rate at the time was just 5.25 percent.

Liquidity Falls

As the price of money jumped, market liquidity evaporated. Until the August 9 squeeze, global financial market liquidity had been at its highest level in at least seventeen years. It had doubled in the previous four years, according to the Bank of England's index, in part because China recycled its trade surplus into the dollar-based financial markets and also restrained consumer prices everywhere by inundating the world with cheap retail goods.

Overnight, the amount of cash available to fuel the debt-powered engines of finance plummeted to a five-year low. Like squirrels amassing nuts to prepare for winter, financial institutions worried that the days of free, easy money might be at their end. Banks began to hoard money rather than lend it out. This amounted to a damning admission: the banking industry had no idea how many off–balance sheet toxic credit instruments would be heading home, but bankers did know that the number and value could be very large indeed. The bigger the cash cushion, in their eyes, the better.

"The effective closure of asset-backed securities and leveraged loan markets left major financial institutions needing to fund growing warehouses of assets that they had not expected to retain on their balance sheets," the Bank of England said in its semi-annual financial stability report, published in October 2007. "Market intelligence suggests banks have stockpiled liquidity to fund the actual and potential expansion of their balance sheets." In other words, a volcano of toxic waste was about to erupt, threatening to drown the banks in a sea of derivatives magma. The smoke was visible to all, and the rumblings underground were growing louder.

A Central Bank Emergency

For the world's central banks, this was a terrifying development. Central banks work to steer individual economies on a stable path between boom and bust by setting borrowing costs at whatever level they deem appropriate. Indeed, the only power they really have is the ability to twitch interest rates higher and lower. When the money markets petrified, central banks risked losing control of interest rates—and economies—unless they acted quickly to restore confidence. An unopposed surge in borrowing costs threatened to strangle the faltering global economy.

With New York markets stirring to life as the day there began, the Frankfurt-based European Central Bank—which oversees monetary policy for the nations that use the euro as their common currency—announced that it would allow banks in its region to borrow as much money as they wanted at a flat rate of 4 percent. The move, it said, was designed to "assure orderly conditions in the euro area money market." Forty-nine banks accepted the offer, borrowing a staggering 95 billion euros that day, which at the time was equivalent to about $130 billion. The Federal Reserve, once it opened for business, followed suit by holding three auctions of overnight money. Banks took $38 billion in total. Canada's central bank also made extra cash available to its banks.

It didn't work. Commercial banks took the cash the central banks offered and hoarded it jealously, sandbagging their perimeters against the deteriorating global economic outlook. With less money circulating, money market rates continued to climb. In the following month, the cost of borrowing dollars for three months soared to 5.73 percent from 5.5 percent, the rate for euros jumped to 4.75 percent from 4.4 percent, and Canada's three-month money market rate spiked to 5.15 percent from 4.76 percent. Borrowing costs, which had previously moved at the stately, measured tempo of a royal procession, raced like amphetamine-fueled sprinters with a finishing line in sight—but the line moved steadily further away.

Borrowed money had spawned entire new species of investments and was the oxygen keeping almost the entire financial system alive. Now the air was getting thinner. Money was scarce for the first time since the beginning of the credit boom. The financial community rapidly recognized the value of breathing deeply and trying not to exhale. Even as banks struggled to produce workable lending rates, they realized that the laws of supply and demand dictated that money could only get more expensive—so they tried to hang on to as much of it as they could lay their hands on.

Bagehot's Blueprint

By pumping billions of dollars, euros, and other currencies into the financial system, the central banks, led by the Fed and the ECB, were doing what the handbook of best monetary practices would have suggested, had such a rulebook existed.

The banks did have a book that came close. Walter Bagehot, editor of *The Economist* from 1861 until his death in 1877, published *Lombard Street: A Description of the Money Markets* in 1873. More than a century later, this seminal study still formed the basis for central banks' attempts to deal with the crisis. "The end is to stay the panic," Bagehot wrote. "Loans should only be made at a very high rate of interest. This will operate as a heavy fine on unreasonable timidity and will prevent the greatest number of applications by persons who do not require it. At this rate, these advances should be made on all good banking securities. The evil is that owing to terror, what is commonly good security has ceased to be so."

Unfortunately for the central banks, the game had changed since Bagehot's day. The new version had a larger number of more entangled players. Modern-day central bankers, moreover, were unwilling to heed Bagehot's urging and demand top-quality collateral for emergency funds. (Toxic collateral, after all, was exactly what banks needed to export from their balance sheets to the warm embrace of the monetary authorities.)

In April 2008, when both the Fed and the Bank of England were lending money against potentially noxious mortgage-backed debt, one of the world's leading former central bankers chastised this relaxation in standards. Paul Volcker was Fed chairman from 1979 to 1987, winning plaudits for his willingness to drive interest rates higher in a bid to squeeze inflation out of the U.S. economy. He told the Economic Club of New York on April 8, 2008, that "a direct transfer of mortgage and mortgage-backed securities of questionable pedigree from an investment bank to the Federal Reserve seems to test the time-honored central bank mantra in times of crisis: lend freely at high rates against good collateral. It tests it to the point of no return."

The central banks ultimately fashioned a money market life support system. It kept banks alive, but at the cost of eventually turning them into a new breed of zombies: monsters addicted to government funds.

Financial firms' failing health and the need to keep money flowing through the economy's arteries and capillaries were two distinct issues that became enmeshed. Rather than keep the money markets alive, central banks might have done better by cutting out that middleman, instead quickly establishing direct government loans to the companies and customers who needed funds. By directing funds through the money markets, the central banks encouraged a logjam. Cash came out of the central banks and got stuck in the banking system, never reaching the intended end users.

Commercial Paper Breakdown

Money market funding costs continued to climb and began to percolate into other financial instruments and out into the broader economy. In yet another example of financial market interconnections, money market turmoil in London provoked chaos in Canada, where investors had no idea how much it should cost to borrow a dollar, a euro, a pound, or even a Canadian dollar.

Canada's $40 billion commercial paper market froze. Investors fled at least seventeen funds, including Coventree Incorporated,

Newshore Financial Corporation, and Quanto Financial Corporation, leaving the group unable to roll over debt and repay lenders. It was the first time in two decades that borrowers in the Canadian commercial paper market had failed to make payments.

The lenders left contemplating losses weren't excitement-seeking speculators. They included companies such as Vancouver-based First Quantum Resources Minerals, which mines for copper in Africa; the Sun-Times, which publishes the *Chicago Sun-Times* newspaper; and Canada Post, which runs the nation's mail service. All three companies had parked spare cash in the commercial paper market to earn more than they could get from bank deposits or government bills, in the belief that commercial paper was a safe investment.

In normal circumstances, it typically was. Commercial paper is a kind of IOU, invented for companies looking to borrow money for ninety days or fewer to meet temporary needs: to cover the gap between buying raw materials to fill a customer order and the customer's full payment, for example. As the finance industry grew more and more promiscuous, however, financial companies began to use the commercial paper market as a new source of short-dated loans to fund longer-dated investments. Their presence contaminated the waters; previously trusted issuers couldn't find new buyers for their debt and so couldn't remain afloat.

Within three weeks of Libor rates going haywire, the cost of borrowing money through the U.S. market for asset-backed commercial paper soared above 6 percent, from 5.32 percent at the start of August. That drove the gap between official overnight interest rates—determined by the Federal Reserve—and the rates companies paid in the real world to its widest level since October 2001. In Europe, the cost of borrowing euros climbed to its highest level in six years, as the desperate scramble for cash superseded the economic backdrop.

The money market freeze exposed a defect in tying other interest rates, such as those for credit cards, to Libor. If they rise or fall with

Libor, payments on $360 trillion in loans and other securities—which may include your car payments or home equity loan—depend ultimately on how much banks trust each other.

That's especially true when times are troubled and that faith is faltering. During times of market stress, the world needs its monetary scaffolding to be as secure as possible; paradoxically, that's exactly when the framework is most vulnerable. That vulnerability can allow financial problems to leak into the wider economy, as they did in this case, with Libor providing a distribution network.

Panic Stations

By August 20, two weeks after Libor began its spike, global financial markets were at "panic stations," according to Stephen King and Richard Cookson, economists at HSBC Holdings in London, which was then Europe's biggest bank by market value. "Should the panic exhibited over the last few days turn into revulsion, the markets may never be the same again," the market watchers wrote in a research report. "Central banks can add liquidity and cut rates, but the world economy is now at risk from financial market seizure."

Central banks' two-part strategy—try to suppress the price of money by making it more cheaply available to the commercial banking industry, and endeavor to increase the supply of money by handing great gobs of cash to the commercial banks—had appeared sensible enough. As it turned out, though, banks' nearly insatiable appetite for stockpiling cash defeated the plan. No matter how hard central banks worked to hand out unprecedented quantities of cash, it disappeared into the financial industry's deep holes, never making its way into the wider economy in the form of consumer or commercial credit.

Public Policy Bends to Markets

By the third quarter of 2007, the global money market was petrified. The monetary authorities, now out of their depth, relied on an ad hoc plan. They would make the moves outlined in their now-outdated playbook, then react on instinct as the credit crunch evolved. For years they had ignored the credit boom, surrendering to the free market. Now the banking community's ruinous behavior would dictate public policy.

The European Central Bank was the first institution to blink. Its officials had all but promised a September rate increase, citing the need for "strong vigilance" against the threat of rising prices— coded language that had presaged eight previous rate increases. When the ECB's governing council members met on September 6 to set regional monetary policy, though, they left the official interest rate unchanged. The cost of borrowing euros had surged to its most expensive in more than six years, and the inflammatory consequences of any move to push official rates higher were deemed too unpredictable. The money market tail was wagging the central bank dog.

U.S. officials were backed into a similar corner. In July, futures market prices suggested that traders and investors were betting that the Fed would keep its official interest rate unchanged. The repercussions of the housing market collapse weren't severe enough for the economy to need the jolt that a rate cut would deliver.

By August, that view had started to flip. Many observers thought money market mayhem would take priority in any discussion of rate changes. "Central banks don't know how to deal with the current situation within the confines of their existing rule books," Patrick Perret-Green, a strategist at Citigroup in London, wrote in a September 4 research report. "The current situation is unprecedented in recent financial history. Rate cuts are inevitable against this background." On September 18, the Fed cut its key interest rate by half a point.

The credit crunch had wrestled the economic reins away from stability's government-appointed guardians.

It's dangerous to cut interest rates in a bid to pacify financial markets, rather than to serve the economy's growth and inflation—and not just because it sets the wrong precedent. Savings account interest is determined by central bank lending rates. Lower official policy rates mean less interest paid to cautious savers, leaving less money in consumers' hands—and less consumer spending to lift the global economy.

Another Great Depression?

For the first time since the crisis began, finance professionals began to evoke the Great Depression. "The loan originations market is in the midst of the most severe dislocation it has seen in years, maybe the most severe since the 1930s," Mark Ernst, the chief executive officer of H&R Block, said on August 30. H&R Block is best known for preparing U.S. income tax returns, but it, too, succumbed to the euphoria of the previous years when it bought a lending company. Now it was bleeding money as it tried to sell the faltering Option One Mortgage Corporation. The U.S. mortgage market's poisonous tentacles had laced throughout the world's financial infrastructure in complex and unpredictable ways.

The housing boom's collapse left a gang of financiers holding defaulted mortgages from families who bought houses they couldn't afford. If that had been the crash's only consequence, the world might easily have emerged relatively unscathed from the credit boom's excesses and expiration. The more reckless lenders would have expired unlamented, a few banks would have gone bust or been forced into mergers, regulators might have started paying more attention to the behavior of the firms they oversee, and consumer spending would have taken a hit for a year or two. The financial community's unrestrained, largely unnoticed overindulgence made that outcome impossible.

SIVs Slither Back onto Bank Balance Sheets

The banking world behaved as it is predisposed to do: bending accounting rules, sometimes nearly to the breaking point; assuming that the future will be just like the past; pursuing profit wherever there was a buck to be made. When turmoil erupted in Libor, increased borrowing costs didn't just make life more expensive for consumers and companies with debts. It also forced banks to reveal even more of their riskier deals, including a whole family of secretive financing techniques called structured investment vehicles.

Structured investment vehicles, known as SIVs, are a bit like virtual banks, built from (no surprise) short-term money borrowed on the commercial paper market and investing in (you guessed it) longer-term, often risky securities, such as collateralized-debt obligations. SIVs make their money on the spread between the lower short-term interest they pay—which is usually close to Libor—and the higher long-term interest they earn. SIVs, which operated as stand-alone companies owned by a larger financial institution, then use those profits make payments to investors who have bought their capital notes, who are also first in line to lose money if the SIV's cash flow can't cover promised payments to all investors.

SIVs were part of the shadow banking system. Entirely legal, they nevertheless operated in a kind of financial underworld, well away from even the most sophisticated investors' radar screens. "I'd never heard of SIVs" before May 2007, said Anthony Bolton, who has run Fidelity International's Special Situations Fund for twenty-eight years (as of 2009) and was the United Kingdom best-known fund manager, in October 2008. "I didn't know they existed."

The rating companies gauged the risks posed by SIVs with the same level of incompetence that informed their collateralized-debt obligation (CDO) business. In July, a Moody's report said that SIVs were "an oasis of calm in the subprime maelstrom" because "the vehicles are not structured to forcibly liquidate assets in times of crisis." Moody's was under the misguided impression that SIVs had plenty of ways to borrow the money they needed to stay afloat. Having those options, the ratings company said, "obviates the need to liquidate large buckets of assets at potentially the worst period in the life of the vehicle."

The money market shutdown proved Moody's wrong. SIVs' business model required borrowing money on the commercial paper market, then borrowing funds again in order to pay off the previous lenders. That wasn't possible in a frozen commercial paper market, and SIVs—pushed into a corner by creditors—began to unload longer-term assets. By the end of August, for example, London-based money manager Cheyne Capital Management Limited told clients it would probably have to dump assets owned by its SIV, the $6 billion Cheyne Finance fund. With the asset-backed commercial paper market frozen, the fund was struggling to finance itself for the next three months. Less than eight weeks later, the SIV had shed 70 percent of its value.

Despite this and similar carnage, most financial professionals only became aware of SIVs on August 21, when Standard & Poor's butchered ratings on $3.2 billion of debt from SIVs spawned by Solent Capital Partners in London and Avendis Group in Geneva. Of that total, S&P slashed $254 million all the way from the top grade—AAA—to CCC+ and CCC. The debt lost sixteen and seventeen ratings levels in a day, their ratings obliterated because the mortgage-backed bonds they owned were degenerating into garbage.

It was a stunning blow to SIV investors. On Tuesday afternoon they owned an AAA-rated asset. By Wednesday morning, that security had dropped to eight levels below investment grade and was now festering in a category defined by S&P as "currently vulnerable to nonpayment."

At first, the SIV shambles looked like just another disaster from a lab full of obscure, complicated financial alchemy. It quickly became clear, however, that SIVs posed a much more insidious risk to the broader system. In essence, the rules governing how much capital banks must set aside to underpin their businesses had an unintended side effect. They encouraged financial institutions to explore ever more creative methods of transferring assets away from their balance sheets. As with every other dodge invented in the credit boom, the banks tested SIVs to the limit, using the structure as a convenient way to keep some of their racier strategies from appearing in their accounts.

This was a completely legal approach, and potentially a clever way to amplify leverage and efficiently manage bank capital. It let an institution expand the total amount of loans it extended without creating a concurrent need to increase the amount of money it put aside to satisfy capital adequacy regulations. SIVs, however, were also completely untested in anything but a near-perfect market environment and, like so many of the clever stratagems promoted during the credit boom, proved to be unsustainable when conditions deteriorated.

The credit-rating companies spent months sifting through the billions of dollars of repackaged bonds and collateralized debt they had merrily hallmarked in earlier years, backtracking on their initial optimism and trying to make amends by re-rating the debt. Now that the grades they had assigned to SIVs were beginning to melt, it was banks' turn to panic. With the money markets shut, no alternative source of funds available, and asset values plunging, the SIVs couldn't stand on their own feet.

Like a college student home for the holidays with a bag full of dirty laundry, the SIVs came slithering back onto the books of the banks that sired them. By the end of the year, the United Kingdom HSBC had absorbed $45 billion of its SIV assets back onto its balance sheet. WestLB and HSH Nordbank, two German institutions, saw $15 billion make its way back home. France's Société Générale was also suckered into bailing out its SIV.

In the United States, Citigroup—credited with inventing SIVs in 1998—had to find space for $58 billion of extra debt in December 2007, after it took responsibility for seven SIVs. Just a month earlier, Citigroup had said that it "will not take actions that will require the company to consolidate the SIVs."

The Citigroup SIVs owned $49 billion in assets, and their composition highlights the deadliness of the derivatives market's rapid deterioration. About 54 percent of the securities began life with top Aaa ratings from Moody's, with 43 percent rated one tier lower, in the Aa category. Only 3 percent of the assets had lower creditworthiness; these were in the A subset.

Those credit ratings, however, had zero defensive capability when valuations plummeted. In rescuing its SIVs, Citigroup assumed responsibility for $10 billion of commercial paper that had an average time to repayment of just 2.4 months, plus $48 billion of medium-term notes with an average maturity of 10.1 months. (The bailout also showed just how heavily SIVs relied on short-term debt to finance their investments.)

Top credit ratings counted for nothing for funds that couldn't borrow against those assets to repay the creditors they had tapped to buy the securities in the first place. With the money markets closed, the credit crunch tightened.

EIGHT

Central Banks, Unbalanced

Caught Off Guard, the Financial Authorities
Make Up the Rules as They Go Along

Central bank independence "is not set in stone."
—Former Federal Reserve chairman Alan Greenspan
in his autobiography, *The Age of Turbulence*

Politicians, not citizens, appoint the specialists who run the world's central banks. Central bankers are typically career civil servants and academics who have spent their entire working lives studying aspects of the economy. They are not entrepreneurs who built businesses, invented products, or worried about having enough money in the company coffers every week to pay workers' salaries.

Central banks have existed for centuries, but their current, dominant role at the heart of the world's largest financial centers is a relatively new, infrequently tested development. Central banks set monetary policy autonomously, without interference from vote-seeking politicians, and this independence is a modern phenomenon, with a track record of only about a decade or so in the United Kingdom and continental Europe. Even in the United States

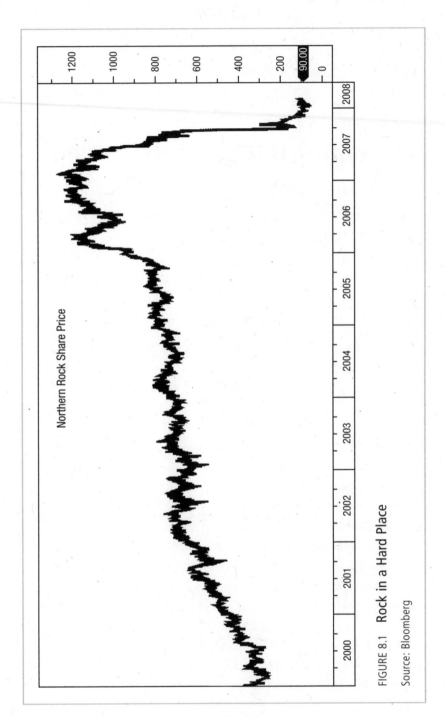

FIGURE 8.1 **Rock in a Hard Place**

Source: Bloomberg

the Treasury could oblige the Federal Reserve to maintain fixed interest rates for both short- and long-term borrowing until the middle of the last century.

In exchange for autonomy, governments and citizens expect central bankers to reveal at least some of the thinking behind their decisions, sharing their insights with the communities they serve. This is an even fresher development, imperfectly executed and something less than a natural inclination for the keepers of the economic flame, no matter how much lip service they pay to the values of clarity and openness.

Despite their seeming independence, the central bankers who tried to fix the credit crisis turned out to be just as malleable and exposed to the shifting sands of public opinion as the politicians who appoint them. As the credit crunch tightened its grip, central bankers ran up against the limits of their alleged autonomy, and their nascent commitment to transparency started to waver.

Not So Rock Solid

The finance industry had been on a borrowing binge for years and now faced a liquidity-free diet. After the money markets froze, the credit crunch was ready for its first poster child: a company big enough to alert global financial watchdogs to the seriousness of the situation, but not so big that its demise would generate economic Armageddon. The crisis was a global one, so an emblematic casualty could have come from anywhere. Indeed, the first one was not American, but from the northernmost part of England. Despite its reassuring name, a regional bank there called Northern Rock was coming undone at the seams.

It is worth taking time to analyze what went wrong with Northern Rock after the money markets closed for business in the third quarter of 2007 because the bank's behavior then, toward the end of its independent existence, embodied all of the hubris, short-sightedness, and vulnerability that modern capitalism embraced during the credit boom. Its denouement also revealed that central bankers were just as unprepared for the unfolding catastrophe as the politicians who appointed them.

Northern Rock traced its roots to 1850, when a group of Newcastle shopkeepers formed a community fund. Newcastle's citizens have a reputation for thriftiness, honesty, and plain talking. The local soccer team, Newcastle United, hasn't won a trophy for years, yet still commands a fanatical following. Players run onto the field in black-and-white striped jerseys emblazoned with the team sponsor's name: Northern Rock. The bank was an archetypal, old-fashioned community lender—until its addiction to bankrolling ambitions with borrowed money backfired spectacularly.

During 2006, Northern Rock increased its share of the U.K. home loan market to 14.5 percent from 12.2 percent; profits grew by more than 50 percent in the second half of that year. Shareholders applauded its apparent success at winning business from its rivals while keeping both costs and default rates under control. Northern Rock's share price climbed by 25 percent in 2006, outpacing every other publicly traded British finance company.

By the middle of 2007, the lender had about 800,000 mortgage customers. In the first half of that year, Northern Rock lent £17.4 billion for home loans, up 37 percent from the year-earlier period. Profit growth, though, started to falter; earnings rose just 0.2 percent in the first half of 2007, as borrowing costs rose faster than income from mortgages.

The bank's flagship offering was the "Together" product, a mortgage that let buyers borrow as much as 125 percent of a property's value. That's not wise lending—but it wasn't Northern Rock's undoing, either. Other U.K. lenders offered mortgages that were equally detached from actual home values.

Moreover, even two months after Northern Rock asked for a government bailout, only 3 percent of the lender's "Together" customers were in arrears, according to company chairman Ron Sandler, and in 2006 the company's bad debts were less than £82 million. "We have low levels of arrears, strong credit-risk management and a low-risk balance sheet," CEO Adam Applegarth, who had spent his entire career at the firm and was the principal architect of its lofty aspirations, said in January 2007. "We do not expect to see a significant deterioration in overall credit quality going forward."

Applegarth was right about the benign state of the company's nonperforming loans, but far too complacent about his balance sheet's composition. Northern Rock's customers weren't the problem. The bank's entire business model—and the borrowed money it relied on—lost viability when the money markets closed. "Life changed on August 9, virtually like snapping a finger," Applegarth said on a September 2007 conference call.

Rapid, aggressive expansion had made Northern Rock the United Kingdom third-biggest mortgage lender, up from fifth in 2006. That growth, though, couldn't rest entirely on its deposits, which totaled just £24.4 billion from 1.4 million checking account customers.

It couldn't ride on mortgage interest revenue, either. Immediately before its demise, the lender was offering customers fixed-rate mortgages costing less than 6.2 percent, according to company press releases issued at the time. Libor money market rates, though, had soared, driving the cost of borrowing British pounds for three months above 6.8 percent—the most expensive level in almost a decade. At the time, Northern Rock paid more for operational financing than it charged borrowers, a pattern that repeated throughout the financial world as the credit boom ended and banks' true risks—and their potential costs—became clearer.

Instead, Northern Rock fueled its growth with funds it borrowed in the money markets. Equity analysts who followed the company knew that more than 70 percent of its funds came from what were called the wholesale markets, where it sold mortgages repackaged into asset-backed bonds and marketed under the reassuring "Granite" brand name.

The conveyor belt, though, had to keep moving, with fresh mortgages created at one end and asset-backed bonds sold at the other. When the money markets froze in August and wholesale funding was no longer available, Northern Rock's strategy of borrowing short to lend long—the same technique on which the entire world of finance relied—was doomed.

Panic on the Streets of Britain

On the evening of September 13, 2007, the British Broadcasting Corporation reported that Northern Rock would get emergency funding from the Bank of England.

By then it was the worst-performing bank on the U.K. stock market for 2007, after losing almost half its market value. Investors finally understood the structural defects in the company's business strategy and had punished Northern Rock's share price accordingly.

The news that Northern Rock needed a handout triggered the first run on a U.K. bank in more than a century. The following morning, thousands of Northern Rock customers lined up outside branch offices all across the country to withdraw their money, with scenes captured live by camera crews and beamed around the nation's television screens. The credit crunch had arrived in Britain's town centers, triggering panic in the streets. In less than four days, Northern Rock customers took back about £2 billion of deposits, according to estimates compiled at the time by analysts at JPMorgan Chase & Company. A run on a bank was the stuff of nightmares. It was fine in the movies, in *Mary Poppins* or *It's a Wonderful Life*. It wasn't supposed to happen in real life, to real people and their real money.

The jig was up. The fragile confidence that serves as the foundation of the relationship between a bank and its depositors evaporated. Northern Rock's executives weren't fraudsters; they hadn't cooked the books, hidden losses, or embezzled money. The company's accounting policies weren't suspect or dodgy; there was no pyramid scheme, no scams or swindles. There was no subterfuge, either, in how the bank achieved its goals: the credit boom had unleashed a wave of liquidity, and Northern Rock surfed the swell in a bid to outpace its competitors, unconstrained by its slender deposit base and unshackled by banking regulations.

That said, neither was Northern Rock a solvent, fully functioning institution that ran into short-term funding difficulties and needed a brief government loan. It was as fundamentally unstable as an SIV or a subprime collateralized-debt obligation, liable to capsize in anything other than ideal conditions.

Moral Hazard

The U.K. authorities could have stood aside and allowed Northern Rock to go bust immediately. Shareholders would have been left with worthless stock; panicking depositors who couldn't withdraw their money quickly enough would have received the statutory compensation allowed under existing deposit guarantee insurance, losing any amount above the reimbursement limit of about £31,700. That would have been unfortunate for the individuals involved, many of whom never stopped to consider whether their money was safe with the Rock, as the bank was affectionately known before its demise.

None of Northern Rock's mortgage customers would have lost their houses as a result of the lender's bankruptcy. Transferring Northern Rock's loans would not have been easy, but the U.K. government could have closed the institution to new business, taken charge of the existing loan book, and held it as an asset until customers either repaid their loans or refinanced with other lenders.

Instead of allowing Northern Rock to fold, though, the Bank of England stepped in with an emergency loan. The government announced that all depositors were fully guaranteed, no matter how much money they had in their accounts. Northern Rock was on the road toward state ownership, and the U.K. taxpayers were on the credit-crunch hook.

Politically, it would have been almost impossible to let Northern Rock's 6,500 employees lose their jobs. Practically, the authorities were terrified that, if they let Northern Rock disintegrate, identical lines of anxious, account-closing customers might form outside another bank, and then another, until customers abandoned the entire banking system. And from a philosophical point of view, authorities in every country where banks floundered had a natural inclination to reach for a sticking plaster. Admitting that life support, transplant surgery, or even euthanasia was a better course for one of the nation's biggest banks would require a fundamental rethink of society's relationship with its financiers—and society wasn't ready for the confessions of failure that would have to accompany such econsiderations.

When governments pledge taxpayers' money to bail out a bank, they cross a line. They create a moral hazard in which there is no reason to curb reckless activities because perpetrators never have to suffer the losses arising from their bad decisions.

Governments have always offered financial institutions an implicit safety net because of finance's potential to wreak economic havoc; once the state makes that guarantee explicit, however, the system loses its ability to moderate future behavior. It's been said that some banks are too big to fail. That idea underwent a subtle transformation as the credit crunch unfolded. A more precise formulation for the future might be that some entities are too risky to fail—which could lead banks to become as risky as possible, to garner maximum protection in the event of a disaster. If a government shields those it rescues from the consequences of their actions, then capitalism loses the Darwinism on which it depends to weed out the unfit and promote the characteristics most likely to survive.

Moreover, government rescues generate private gains for the executives and shareholders of the companies involved. The rewards remain in those private hands, but the costs and eventual shortfalls are public losses, borne by society as a whole. The pleasures are enjoyed by the few, while the pain is shared among the many. It is hard to think of a less desirable outcome.

Refusing Responsibility

Policy makers knew it was dangerous to offer unlimited, after-the-fact guarantees to institutions that had sailed too close to the wind and were starting to sink. They failed, though, to acknowledge that the financial services industry's breakneck growth was breeding behemoths that would run amok if and when they broke free from the slim regulatory chains that supposedly bound them.

Central bankers also underestimated how hard it would be to maintain the courage of their capitalist convictions as the credit crash tested their resolve to avoid interfering in financial markets' free operations. The stakes had grown too high, oversight had been too lax for too long, and central banks had washed their hands of any responsibility for wrestling with equity, real estate, or security asset prices.

With hindsight, central bankers' refusal to take any responsibility for controlling asset prices seems misguided. The cliché that central bankers are there to take away the punch bowl when revelers get too rowdy contains a core truth. It doesn't make them popular, but central bankers do have a duty to shut down the bar. It's part and parcel of their independence. They have the freedom to take politically uncomfortable and unpopular stances. It's inherently difficult to know when rising prices create a bubble, of course, but the challenge doesn't negate central banks' obligation to try to prevent bursting bubbles from wrecking the economy.

Alan Greenspan's Federal Reserve might have done more to try to dissuade investors from bidding U.S. equities to the peak prices seen at the beginning of the decade. U.S. interest rates could have risen faster earlier when it was clear that a 1 percent borrowing cost had done enough to stimulate the economy and avert deflation. And central bankers might have found some nuanced language to warn house buyers, mortgage lenders, and politicians of the dangers of an unrestrained housing market bubble.

Some market watchers absolve central banks on the grounds that the financial markets and broader economy may be largely independent of central banks' actions, in good times and bad. Even these apologists, however, must admit that monetary policy experts failed to appreciate the banking community's newfound daring—which appeared as industry rules allowed banks to set aside less and less capital to fund their most outlandish escapades—and the potential consequences of an enforced borrowing hiatus.

A lack of capital is different from a liquidity shortage. The former is about ability; the latter is about willingness. Central banks can ease a liquidity squeeze by making more money available, enough to ensure a surplus that can spill out of banks and into the pipelines to companies and consumers. When banks have insufficient capital, however, extra central bank money just disappears into the balance sheet. Because financial firms had been allowed to play the markets and accrue liabilities for years without any corresponding increase in the capital they set aside, closed money markets and the ensuing credit squeeze left central banks without a workable plan to defeat the crisis.

King's Flip-Flop

On September 12, the day before the BBC broke the news of Northern Rock's rescue, Bank of England governor Mervyn King gave a speech outlining how the U.K. central bank planned to discharge its duties. Making emergency funds available to banks is a bad idea, King said, because it "encourages excessive risk-taking, and sows the seeds of a future financial crisis." If commercial lenders know that the government will always save the institution in the end, then those bankers will make riskier choices than they might without a safety net.

The U.K. central bank chief also said that helping commercial banks salvage their "risky or reckless lending" is especially dangerous because it "encourages the view that as long as a bank takes the same sort of risks that other banks are taking, then it is more likely that their liquidity problems will be insured ex post by the central bank." Government guarantees instill a herd mentality among bankers, promoting the notion that there's safety in numbers. King's stance seemed clear: the central bank would not underwrite licentious bank lending.

Two days later, though, King agreed to lend Northern Rock an unspecified amount of money to prevent it from crashing. A week after that, the central bank started accepting damaged mortgage-backed bonds as loan collateral, allowing commercial banks and mortgage lenders to exchange their spoiled assets for top-rated government securities.

These were either admirable decisions to put duty before dogma and pragmatism over philosophy, or an embarrassing U-turn by an academic economist warned that the ice beneath his unelected feet was wearing uncomfortably thin.

Market analysts knew that the government was due to decide whether to reappoint King to another four-year term as governor. "King appears to have blinked at the first sign of real political pressure," Christopher Wood, a strategist at CLSA Limited in Hong Kong, wrote in a research note published at the time. Wood noted that the governor had done "precisely what King claimed he was determined not to do, for fear of encouraging a future financial crisis."

Quizzed by politicians at a televised Treasury Select Committee meeting on September 20, 2007, King looked as if he hadn't slept for weeks. A bank run really *was* the stuff of central banking nightmares, it seemed.

When asked whether the government had leaned on him to change his mind, lend money to Northern Rock, and allow other banks to dump faulty mortgage bonds on the central bank, King dodged the question. He vowed that his decisions had not been influenced by any external pressure, without saying whether the government had made demands. "I give you my personal assurance that I would never do anything unless I thought that it was the right thing to do," King said. "Independence is not just about legislation, it's about having people in the bank who will do the right thing and not just what people ask them to do."

Reverting to Secrecy

That same meeting revealed that King had tried to find a different way to rescue Northern Rock without offering open-ended backing. King told the politicians grilling him that he would have favored a secret rescue of the mortgage company, without depositors or shareholders knowing that Northern Rock had been forced to seek state aid. Other financial institutions would also have been in the dark, of course, so they would not have expected additional rescues. A set of laws introduced in previous years, in particular a 2005 ruling on market transparency, had made such a clandestine salvage operation illegal, King said.

"The bank would have preferred to have acted covertly as lender of last resort, to have lent to Northern Rock without publishing it," King told the politicians. "As a result of the market abuses directive, we were unable to carry that out." It was an astonishing admission. Had the Bank of England's lawyers given the all-clear, the central bank would have mounted a furtive maneuver to channel taxpayers' money to Northern Rock.

Clearly, central banks were making up policy as they went along. Cloak-and-dagger salvage operations, using public money to bolster private institutions, have no place in a modern democracy.

A similar situation arose in the United States By early 2009, the Federal Reserve had committed at least $1.5 trillion of national aid to banks through eleven different lending programs, but refused to reveal either the recipients of that assistance or what securities it had taken as collateral guarantees. The Fed contested Bloomberg News efforts to secure those disclosures using freedom of information laws. Central bankers have a powerful, instinctive urge toward secrecy, it seems—one that they would be better off resisting.

CEOs Pay the Price

As 2007 entered its final quarter, market conditions continued to deteriorate. The Bank for International Settlements calculates that between October 11 and 19, Moody's and Standard & Poor's cut credit ratings on more than 2,500 subprime mortgage bonds, worth a combined total of more than $80 billion.

The banks were forced to write off more and more of their toxic assets, and the blame game began, with the all-too-predictable twist that Wall Street chose to reward failure with yet more oversized payouts. Stanley O'Neal lost his job as chief of Merrill Lynch in October 2007; Charles Prince, his counterpart at Citigroup, followed in November. Neither went voluntarily or accepted any blame for the disaster. Instead, O'Neal and Prince experienced the modern equivalent of being pushed off a ledge—albeit with a $161.5 million golden parachute to break O'Neal's fall, and about $60 million to cushion Prince.

More and more financial corners were being poisoned by "the stench of banks not coming clean with their subprime exposures in the first place," as the credit strategy team at Société Générale said in a November 2007 report. Something was rotten in the markets.

NINE

Et Tu, Money Markets and Municipals?

The Crunch Catches Vanilla Investments

*It is a little too easy to blame the present situation on an accumulation
of individual greed, exemplified by bankers or brokers, and to lose sight
of the fact that governments committed to deregulation and the en-
couragement of speculation and high personal borrowing were elected
in Britain and the United States for a crucial couple of decades.*
— ROWAN WILLIAMS, ARCHBISHOP OF CANTERBURY, IN
SPEECH MADE IN CARDIFF, WALES, ON MARCH 7, 2009

FINANCIAL MANIAS ARE NOT a new development. In 1636 and 1637,
the Netherlands was gripped by tulip mania. The price of the most
prized tulip bulb, for a flower known as Semper Augustus, trebled in
three years to 6,000 guilders, at a time when a small town house
might cost about 300 guilders.

Then as now, the bulbs produced only flowers. They had no
magical powers, didn't cure disease or have desirable chemical properties, couldn't satisfy the hunger of a continent or hydrate a desert.
Nevertheless, bulbs changed hands in a classic example of the

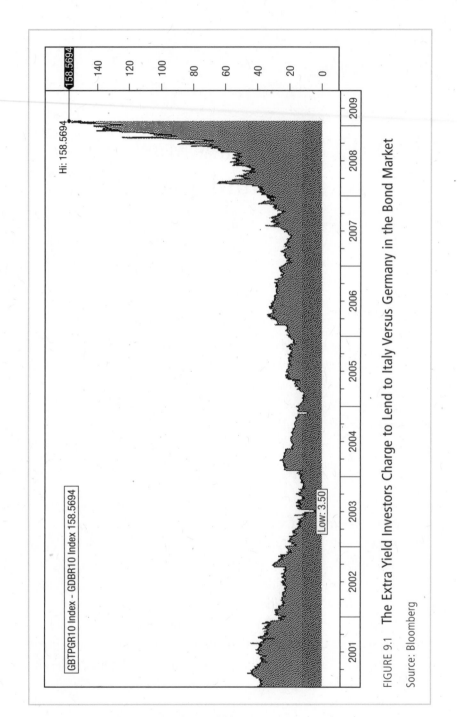

FIGURE 9.1 The Extra Yield Investors Charge to Lend to Italy Versus Germany in the Bond Market

Source: Bloomberg

greater fool theory: purchasers knew that they would always turn a profit because, no matter how much they paid, a bigger idiot would later pay even more. As Edward Chancellor detailed in his 1999 book *Devil Take the Hindmost*, traders paid for bulbs using IOUs in a futures market called the *windhandel*, or wind trade, because the bulbs were still growing in the ground and couldn't physically change hands.

"By the later stages of the mania, the fusion of the 'windhandel' with paper credit created a perfect symmetry of insubstantiality; most transactions were for tulip bulbs that could never be delivered because they didn't exist and were paid for with credit notes that could never be honored because the money wasn't there," Chancellor wrote. "On 3 February 1637, the tulip market suddenly crashed. There was no clear reason for the panic except that spring was approaching when delivery fell due and the game would be up."

Incredible as it may seem, the more recent credit boom infected the allegedly sophisticated world of modern finance with a similar obsession, albeit for leverage and derivatives rather than for fledgling flowers. Tulip mania, though, lasted for just two years; the credit boom endured for more than a decade, allowing ample time for the craze to insinuate itself into every corner of the global economy. Institutions' passion for pursuing better returns through leverage and risky investments wasn't confined to exotic corners of the investment terrain. Even simple, easily understood investment classes became quagmires of distrust, downgrade, and destabilization as the financial fabric unraveled.

Money Market Funds Break the Buck

In the ten weeks ending in mid-October 2007, total U.S. investor appetite for asset-backed commercial paper—a key source of funds for structured investment vehicles—had shrunk by 24 percent, to a little less than $900 billion. The best estimates available at the time suggested that SIVs owned about $320 billion in deteriorating assets.

SIVs' abrupt demise—which quickly followed their inability to sell commercial paper—revealed another uncomfortable truth about the pervasive craze for complexity. The U.S. authorities realized that ordinary citizens, regular folks building nest eggs through saving, were among the lenders who had helped fund SIVs' explosive growth. These vulnerable retail investors had extended loans that were now in big trouble, all because they had put cash in money market funds.

Before their role in the credit crash, money market funds were widely considered a very safe, conservative investment. Offering returns at rates that are just a bit higher than those of a savings account, money market accounts are not insured but are still suitable for widows and orphans. Give a dollar to a money market fund, and at the very least the fund will return a whole dollar—ideally, with the little interest payment that usually accompanies a very small amount of risk.

To deliver that risk-free return, money market funds typically limit themselves to mundane investments: Treasury bills, commercial paper, and certificates of deposit. To maximize the likelihood of repayment, they buy debt with short maturities.

This very vanilla investment book had earned money market fund managers a nearly blemish-free reputation. Only one money market fund had ever failed to repay its investors every dollar assigned to its care, a scenario known as "breaking the buck." The fund, Community Bankers U.S. Government Money Market Fund, went bust in 1994 after investing 43 percent of its $82 million in a kind of structured note called adjustable-rate securities. Community Bankers bet wrongly that interest rates would not rise; the fund lost 4 cents of every invested dollar.

That single disaster had never been repeated, and money market funds enjoyed a stoutly defended reputation for safety. In 1995, at least four financial companies ploughed their own money into their money market funds, defending investors from losses and ensuring that the buck remained unbroken. (Poor investment decisions caused the losses, in this case.)

But floods of liquidity were seeping into every part of the financial markets, and some money market fund managers were tempted. What if they could maintain that sterling reputation, follow their fund rules, and still deliver returns that would beat the competition and lure new investors? The better their returns, the more money flowed in and the bigger the fees they could generate—and the more they could pay themselves. It was the same behavioral pattern seen repeatedly throughout the finance industry.

Some of the riskier money market funds began to place the word "enhanced" in their fund titles. It's unlikely that investors knew how managers would achieve that enhancement, and they certainly didn't expect that managers would bet 20 cents of each hard-earned dollar on the 33:1 outsider running in that day's afternoon horse race. That, however, is a fair approximation of what many U.S. money market funds did with the money entrusted to them.

Supercharged Returns—and a Supercharged Disaster

By the third quarter of 2007, U.S. money market mutual funds controlled more than $2.9 trillion, an increase of almost 50 percent in two years, according to the Investment Company Institute, the mutual fund industry trade group. As in so many other markets, as more cash became available, money managers became increasingly willing to make riskier bets.

Money market funds could buy only debt scheduled for repayment in no more than thirteen months and needed an average time to repayment—across all holdings—of 90 days or fewer. Even so, they found ways to supercharge returns, typically by stretching their debt-selection criteria to include the flavors of commercial paper they were willing to buy. Collateralized-debt obligations (CDOs) often sold commercial paper as part of the short-term debt they used to pay for investments, and they tapped money market funds as buyers.

Buying subprime collateralized-debt obligations was still off limits to money markets. Buying asset-backed commercial paper issued by an SIV or CDO with a top AAA credit rating, though, was entirely legitimate, even though both strategies exposed investors to the same risk. Just as in the derivatives industry, acceptable credit ratings allowed investors to buy securities without doing their own analysis of how much money those investments might lose, given a change in circumstances.

Funds' investment rules were just loose enough to let managers get into trouble. As a result, money market funds grew entangled with CDOs and SIVs. That, in turn, threatened the economic well-being of the regular folks who seeded money market funds with their nest eggs, and who would have run a mile from anything as opaque and convoluted as a structured investment vehicle up to its eyeballs in collateralized debt and derivatives.

M-LEC: First of the Acronym Rescue Attempts

Appalled that disastrously performing SIVs could force money market funds to break the buck, the U.S. Treasury intervened. In October 2007, it forced Citigroup, Bank of America, and JPMorgan to establish a new investment vehicle: the snappily named Master Liquidity Enhancement Conduit. M-LEC, the first in a long series of government-issued financial lifeboats, was designed to stop collapsing SIVs from pulling down money market funds that had lent money unwisely.

In this plan, M-LEC would revive the commercial paper market by selling securities backed by the three investment banks' full faith and credit. The move would reopen the market, and M-LEC proceeds would help the three banks buy existing SIV assets, such as subprime mortgage bonds, easing SIVs' plight and building a firebreak to protect money market funds.

The plan failed, as did subsequent government rescue efforts, on attempts to discover an underlying value for securities that had become essentially worthless, with little prospect of recovery. A company, with assets, revenue, and market position, typically has an underlying, intrinsic value. A collateralized-debt obligation, by contrast, is worth only what someone else will pay for it—and few were willing to pay much for CDOs as the credit crunch continued and underlying debt defaulted.

Market commentators smelled a rat. The M-LEC plan seemed to simply add another layer to the pyramid scheme. It offered no way to address the underlying issue: values for SIV-owned securities were plunging. "It looks as if the banks are really trying to create value via financial engineering when there is not a way to create such value via this game of musical chairs," Nouriel Roubini, the economics professor at New York University's Stern School of Business, wrote in a research note at the time. "The entire scheme seems like one that can work only if banks fully recognize now the losses on their SIV assets—in which case there is no need for this complex plan as assets can be disposed of at low prices today. If such losses are not allowed to be recognized, the scheme cannot work."

Like many government-led rescue attempts, M-LEC could succeed only if CDO prices eventually recovered. What's more, it appeared to support the pretense that prices hadn't fallen as low as they really had, propping up SIVs so that they wouldn't dump damaged assets into the market at whatever price they could get.

"M-LEC seems to be designed not just to avoid fire sales but also to prevent price discovery," wrote Bernard Connolly, chief global strategist at American International Group's Banque AIG unit in London, in a research note. "It stinks, as does the Treasury's sponsorship of the scheme. But the state of financial markets and of the global economy is such that the authorities and market participants around the world are going to have to hold their noses."

By March 2009, SIVs had defaulted on more than $30 billion of debt, hammering the investors—including many money market funds—that lent them money. Many companies, including Bank of America, Legg Mason, SEI Investments, and SunTrust Banks, opted to bail out their money market funds individually, absorbing losses in order to make investors whole. In March 2009, for example, Legg Mason announced that it had dumped the final $1.8 billion of SIV securities it bought for its money market funds, thereby taking a 75 percent loss. Legg Mason waited more than a year to abandon SIVs after it first revealed its SIV investments in November 2007. The delay cost the firm about $1.7 billion in after-tax losses, more than any other asset manager with money in SIVs.

Monolines' Thin Capital Cushions

Its principals abandoned M-LEC as unworkable just before Christmas 2007, less than two months after beginning it. By then, another seemingly drab panel in the financial patchwork was proving a little too colorful for comfort.

Few trillion-dollar businesses are as dull as those in the monoline industry, which help municipalities borrow money by guaranteeing state and city bonds. As 2007 ended, MBIA was the world's biggest bond insurer, by amount of debt insured, followed by Ambac Financial Group. Other industry specialists included Security Capital Assurance, Assured Guaranty, CIFG Guaranty, and Financial Guaranty Insurance.

Monoline customers are typically local governments that want to borrow money but lack the top credit scores that would let them pay bond buyers the lowest possible interest rates. To pay the lowest rate, a local government pays a bond insurer—which does have the benefit of a top credit rating—to guarantee bond repayment, allowing the bond issuer to pay investors a lower interest rate. (The arrangement is a bit like asking a friend to cosign a retail loan or lease. The cosigner must repay the loan—or the rent—if the primary borrower or renter defaults.) Even after paying that fee, municipalities typically borrow funds more cheaply than they could have without the monoline company's help. As long as a monoline has enough capital set aside, it can guarantee multiple bond issues without undermining its credit rating.

By 2007, monolines had guaranteed more than $1 trillion in bonds, including asset-backed debt, sold by U.S. cities and states. Municipal bonds, though, proved too prosaic, even for the monolines. They decided to spice up their lives—and their incomes—with some side action in derivatives. Monolines rented out their AAA credit ratings to the collateralized-debt market, guaranteeing the repayment of about $100 billion of CDOs that wouldn't otherwise have achieved a top credit grade.

Monolines wrote those guarantees when CDO defaults seemed unlikely, and the fee income looked like easy money. Now, though, CDOs' slumping values and the rising risk of nonpayment made it increasingly likely that investors would ask the monolines to make good on their pledges. That would deplete monoline firms' capital and endanger their own ratings.

A monoline without a top credit rating is about as useful as a chocolate teapot. Such a firm couldn't offer new clients a top credit rating, and any existing debt guaranteed by that company would slip down the credit rating scale, eroding its value. Monolines' greed embroiled local government debt in the subprime scandal. The credit crunch was far from reaching its conclusion. On the contrary: it was spreading.

As November 2007 began, Fitch Ratings investigated whether CDOs' dwindling creditworthiness would force bond insurers to raise additional capital in order to bolster their balance sheets and preserve their top ratings. "The rating agencies can hardly bury their heads in the sand and they will most likely have to act," Geraud Charpin, UBS's London-based head of credit strategy, said in a November 6 report. "If the bonds of the monolines are downgraded below AAA, many holders will be forced to sell and monolines would lose their ability to wrap municipal debt. A politically engineered solution will ensure an acceptable way out where the innocent pensioner does not lose out and states are able to continue funding themselves and build more roads, schools, etc."

Ken Zerbe, an analyst at Morgan Stanley, questioned whether bond insurers still had a viable business model. The likely default surge, after all, would deplete their capital to unhealthily low levels. Ambac, the second-biggest bond insurer, responded in November 2007 by saying that there were "many misconceptions" about its finances. By then, its shares had shed almost 70 percent of their value in less than a year. (In general, any time a financial company suggests the market has misunderstood its business, or that its critics have misinterpreted its situation, investors should run for the hills. If a company's operations are beyond the comprehension of an analyst at a major investment bank, the problem is likely with the business's structure and explanations— not with the analyst.)

Because they had made a $100 billion gamble on the collateralized-debt market's continuing health, bond insurers found themselves in the same brittle, unstable state as the rest of the financial world: without enough capital set aside to withstand systemic shocks.

In the equity markets, shareholders demand that executives manage companies as efficiently as possible. In practice, that typically means using as little capital as possible. Capital is expensive, and regulatory authorities have the power to make it even more costly by imposing higher capital adequacy standards on companies taking big risks.

In the credit markets, however, financial companies didn't put aside enough capital to cover the risks they were taking, and regulators didn't move to correct the situation until it was too late. Insuring a collateralized-debt obligation in a young, untested market was clearly a much more unpredictable proposition than providing surety for municipal bonds, which are usually designed to fund a specific infrastructure project and are backed by municipal taxes and revenue. The bond insurers, though, did not increase their capital bases to match higher risk levels. The cushions were too thin when the ride got rocky.

Credit Ratings Drop—Again

In the end, the stock market and credit-rating companies belatedly applied sanctions for that under-allocation of capital. The equity market punishment came in the form of plunging stock prices for monolines. The credit-rating companies slashed monolines' enterprise-wide ratings, albeit tardily, and with a substantial amount of kicking and screaming from the monolines.

In March 2008, Fitch found the courage to say that it was considering cutting MBIA's AAA credit rating. MBIA responded by writing to Fitch and demanding that it withdraw the assessment, and return or destroy any of the private information that MBIA had provided to facilitate the assessment. MBIA was battling to avoid the fate of its smaller rival, Ambac Financial Group, which had seen its rating cut by two grades to AA two months earlier, undermining the value of the $556 billion in debt it insured.

Fitch came out fighting. Company CEO Stephen Joynt asked MBIA bluntly if its request was because "we are continuing our analytical review and may conclude that, in our view, MBIA's insurer financial strength is no longer AAA."

At the end of the month, Joynt told the insurer that Fitch would continue to provide investors with its view on MBIA's creditworthiness, even without MBIA's assistance—or its fees. Fitch cited its duty to protect bondholders. "If we withdraw our rating, they may be forced sellers," Joynt said in a press statement. "Maintaining a rating—whether AAA or even if downgraded to AA category—continues the recognition of the high quality of their investment."

In June 2008, Fitch backed down and withdrew its grading. Moody's, however, slashed MBIA's rating by five levels that month, down to A2 from Aaa. The change triggered clauses requiring the monoline to pay its insurance customers $7.4 billion in collateral and other fees, compensating them for the newly degraded status of insurance contracts they had with MBIA.

Worldwide Recession Fears

As credit crunch contagion spread, more economic alarm bells began to ring. By the end of November, the Deutsche Bank economics team, led from New York by chief economist Peter Hooper, was talking seriously about a worldwide recession. "For the global economy as a whole, the odds for a mild recession are a little less than one-half, those for a more significant recession are about one-in-three," the team wrote in a research report.

Price signals from the bond and money markets suggested an ever-worsening dislocation, one that traders and investors bet would force central banks to defend their economies by lowering official interest rates.

Libor rates were still broken, with banks charging each other 5 percent to borrow dollars for three months. That meant debt payments for companies and consumers were still increasing, not diminishing. U.S. government bonds, though, were yielding less than 4.5 percent for thirty years, less than 4 percent for ten years, and below 3 percent for government debt repayable in two years. Even so, the Federal Reserve's policy rate, typically the lowest level in the suite of U.S. government-related borrowing costs, was still 4.5 percent in November 2007.

In continental Europe, the euro's introduction reduced borrowing costs for governments that adopted the common currency. Because all the debt was denominated in the same currency, interest costs had converged to the lower levels enjoyed by the most economically respected governments, such as Germany, rather than to the higher costs previously paid by less creditworthy nations, including Italy.

By November 2007, though, investors charged Italy 4.44 percent to borrow for ten years, compared with the 4.06 percent charged to Germany—the widest spread since March 2001. Compared with Germany, Spain was also paying its highest premium in almost six years. The moves suggested that shared currency is a pale substitute for a sustained track record for economic vigilance, which Germany enjoys, and is no panacea for repeated bouts of fiscal negligence, the charge Italy faced. Individual nations were still responsible for repaying government debt in the euro zone. Investors didn't make decisions about the region as a whole; instead, they cast their votes on individual European Union members, picking winners and potential losers.

The corporate bond market, meanwhile, was shut. In 2006, investors bought more than €29 billion of high-yield, high-risk debt from companies in the European market. That was almost as much as they purchased in the previous two years combined, according to figures compiled by Suki Mann, a London-based credit strategist at Société Générale.

In the first six months of 2007, bond buyers spent more than €24 billion on fresh debt. When the money markets froze in August, however, companies found that investors no longer wanted their bonds. No high-yield debt changed hands in August, September, October, November, or December 2007, Mann's figures show. Investors wouldn't lend low-grade companies money in such an uncertain economy, no matter how high the yields on offer.

Embarrassing Rescue Attempts

The unraveling market for euro-area bonds, the decline in U.S. Treasury yields, and the closure of Europe's high-yield bond market reflected what investors call a flight to quality: money moving away from risk and toward seemingly less dangerous investments. Entrusting money to the U.S. and German governments began to look like the wisest course of action, as money managers adopted a "safety first" approach. Investors lost so much trust in the financial system that, by December 2008, they were willing to accept negative yields on three-month Treasury bills. Negative yields meant investors paid for the privilege of lending money to the U.S. government because at least their capital, if not their income, was considered safe there.

Investors' confidence in the global financial architecture was degenerating so rapidly that central banks could not get ahead of the game, no matter how many billions they pumped in to support the system. No commercial bank wanted the public to know it needed central bank support. To remove that stigma, in August the Fed persuaded Citigroup, Bank of America, JPMorgan, and Wachovia to each borrow $500 million at its discount window.

The stigma, however, remained. Banks continued to shun help for fear of being punished for a confessed capital shortage. Meanwhile in the United Kingdom the Bank of England held a series of auctions for three-month money, and no one showed up. The banks felt that their need to keep up appearances outweighed their need for cash.

As commercial banks grew more fearful for their reputations, central banks found that their key policy tools for maintaining control of borrowing costs were emasculated. "This poses a question about the social contract between the authorities and the banking system, where central banks provide funds in unlimited quantities against collateral but at a penal rate," Paul Tucker, the Bank of England policy maker with responsibility for monitoring markets, said in

November. "If it's stigmatized to draw those funds, then there is a question about how the system will function over the future."

From Liquidity Scare to Solvency Worries

The Fed met every six weeks to contemplate its next move; the European Central Bank and the Bank of England did the same on a monthly basis. Traders and investors, though, delivered judgment every second of every minute of every day, with each bit of fresh evidence pointing to a deeper catastrophe.

The crisis of confidence that gripped the money markets in August, prompting banks to start hoarding capital, underwent a subtle, damning twist: concerns about solvency began to replace worries about liquidity, making the situation even more dangerous.

"It's not so much that people are worried about the amount of total losses in the subprime market," Bank of England governor Mervyn King said in November. "There is genuine concern about what might happen to the capital position of the banks." A month later, King said he detected "a palpable sense of fear in financial markets about the capital position of banks." Fear, not greed, was now in charge of the global financial rollercoaster.

TEN

Giants Fall

The Credit Crisis Reaches Its Climax

Owners of capital will stimulate the working class to buy more and more of expensive goods, houses and technology, pushing them to take more and more expensive credits, until their debt becomes unbearable. The unpaid debt will lead to bankruptcy of banks, which will have to be nationalized, and State will have to take the road which will eventually lead to communism.

—KARL MARX, *DAS KAPITAL*, 1867

IN THE EARLY PART of the 1990s, the most important companies in the United States were those that relied on discretionary consumer spending. McDonald's and Walt Disney are two good examples. Measured by their stock market values, in 1993 this industry group accounted for 16 percent of the Standard & Poor's Index of the 500 biggest U.S. companies.

Industrial companies that bashed metal into various shapes or moved earth from place to place were the second-most important group, comprising 14 percent of the index, followed by a 12 percent

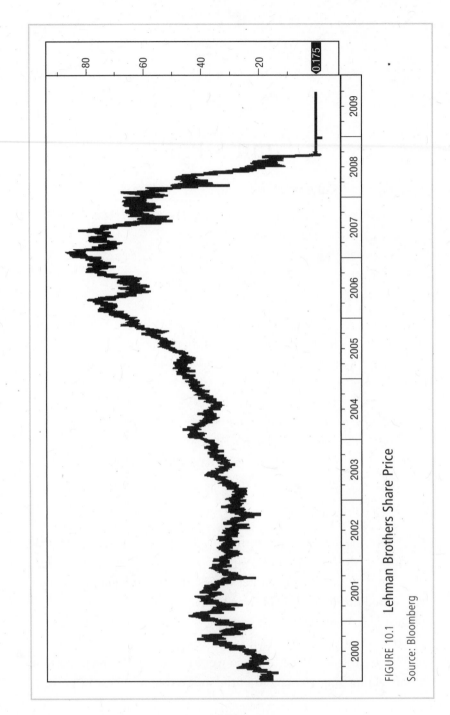

FIGURE 10.1 Lehman Brothers Share Price

Source: Bloomberg

index share for companies that made staple goods such as foods and medicines. Only 11 percent of the S&P 500's total market capitalization came from banks, insurance companies, and the like. Finance facilitated other business. It was not itself a primary objective.

Banking Moves Out of Its Box

Fast forward fifteen years, and the picture looks very different. By the middle of 2008, financial firms had dominated America's corporate landscape for three years, contributing about 20 percent of the S&P 500 index. (The technology industry was a distant second, at about 15 percent.) Bankers enjoyed near rock-star status, mostly because the gargantuan incomes they paid themselves came with yachts, private jets, expensive cars, and many of the other trappings of a rock-star lifestyle. "Finance is supposed to be a service industry, an aid to the business of genuine wealth creation," says Sean Corrigan, who oversees more than $8 billion as chief investment strategist at Diapason Commodities Management in Lausanne, Switzerland. "Once we accord banks the sort of overblown importance they have enjoyed this past quarter of a century, we become hostage to the megalomania of their executives and head traders."

Unfettered banking industry growth created a great deal of wealth, so no one was in a hurry to reverse the trend. Jim Reid, a London-based credit strategist for Deutsche Bank, calculates that the U.S. financial sector made what he calls "excess" profits worth an incredible $1.2 trillion in the ten years between June 1998 and June 2008. Reid compared financial firms' annual profit growth to what they might have earned had their profit increased in parallel with the overall economy, which expanded by 64 percent during that period. The leverage-fueled financial sector grew by nearly 250 percent.

It wasn't until June 2008 that bank shares' slumping prices diminished the financial industry's weighting to less than 16 percent of the S&P 500 index. Computer and software makers such as Apple and Microsoft were the new leaders, with more than 16.5 percent of the benchmark. Banking shrunk, however, only after the credit crunch already exacted a high price from society.

By the time Reid published his analysis in a July 2008 research report, U.S. firms had written off almost $190 billion of the value of their deteriorating securities. "One could come to the conclusion that there is another $1 trillion of value destruction to go," Reid wrote. Reid was prescient; by September 2008, write-downs stood at $507 billion. By April 2009, they had reached $1.3 trillion. The banking world gave back everything it had earned during the boom—and more.

A Repeat Performance

It wasn't the first time the banking fraternity had made and then lost a ton of money on an exotic escapade. More than two decades ago, Latin American countries, including Mexico and Brazil, defaulted on their debts, leaving U.S. banks with stacks of unpaid loans. "In the summer of 1982, large American banks lost close to all their past earnings (cumulatively), about everything they ever made in the history of American banking—everything," Nassim Nicholas Taleb wrote in *Black Swan*. "They had been lending to South and Central American countries that all defaulted at the same time—'an event of an exceptional nature.' So it took just one summer to figure out that this was a sucker's business and that all their earnings came from a very risky game. All the while the bankers led everyone, especially themselves, into believing that they were 'conservative.' They are not conservative; just phenomenally skilled at self-deception by burying the possibility of a large, devastating loss under the rug."

Investors, ignorant of the dangers and seduced by seemingly endless profit, bid up financial stocks. Because bank balance sheets were so opaque, however, investors effectively bought into "blind pools" of assets and liabilities. What you don't know can hurt you, as investors discovered in 2008, when toxic assets were revealed.

Bear Bailed Out

During the same year, the Fed and the Treasury made a series of interlinked decisions that made both the climax and the aftermath of the credit crunch much, much worse than they might otherwise have been.

First, the U.S. authorities underwrote a Bear Stearns bailout. That saved the brokerage from bankruptcy, albeit at the cost of its independence. Then the government declined to offer Lehman Brothers similar assistance when it ran out of road, preferring instead to watch from the sidelines as the biggest bankruptcy in history unfolded.

Finally, within days of Lehman's failure, the Fed and the Treasury were forced into a 180-degree policy shift. The imminent collapse of American International Group (AIG) threatened to unleash financial Armageddon—so regulators signed over taxpayer money to plug gaping holes in the insurance company's swollen derivatives business.

Individually, each decision made sense at the time it was made. Collectively, however, the authorities' flip-flop—salvation, abandonment, then salvation again—obliterated investors' remaining confidence in the financial system. Moral hazard—the idea that people fully exposed to a risk may act differently than those who are insulated from the same risk—went from a theoretical concern to a practical consideration. Why lose money in order to cut ties with Lehman if the government will step in, as it did for Bear Stearns, when the going gets rough? And after the government did not rescue Lehman, why trust an implicit government guarantee ever again?

To be fair, financial authorities were up against all the elements that contributed to the credit crunch: bank cannibalism, transient liquidity, broken business models masquerading as corporate structures, and regulators' failure to quickly notice and solve problems.

They also faced a quickly deteriorating situation. Bear Stearns, for instance, went from solvent to endangered at near-warp speed. Reporters asked U.S. Securities and Exchange Commission chairman Christopher Cox on March 11, 2008, if he was concerned about Bear Stearns' financial condition. "We have a good deal of comfort about the capital cushions at these firms at the moment," Cox responded. The following day, chief executive officer Alan Schwartz told CNBC that the firm's "liquidity cushion" was sufficient to weather market fluctuations, with his company's $17 billion cash position unchanged since the end of November. None of his customers were shunning Bear, Schwartz said. "We have direct dealings with all of these institutions, and we have active markets going with each one, and our counterparty risk has not been a problem," he said.

That confidence was short-lived. Brokers, futures traders, collateral managers and compliance officers ranked counterparties from weakest to strongest and pulled back from doing business with the most fragile. Fairly or unfairly, some of the same names appeared on multiple lists, spelling "game over" for the accused.

In the space of just two days, clients—including hedge funds—withdrew $17 billion from Bear Stearns accounts. Due to "rumors that were untrue," banks wouldn't lend to Bear Stearns even if it put up "relatively liquid" assets as collateral, Bear Stearns chief financial officer Samuel Molinaro said on a March 14 conference call with analysts and investors. "We have tried to confront and dispel these rumors and parse fact from fiction," Schwartz added. "Nevertheless, amidst this market chatter, our liquidity position in the last twenty-four hours had significantly deteriorated."

Emergency Funding and a Shotgun Wedding

The Federal Reserve decided it couldn't let the securities firm collapse. Bear's available liquidity had evaporated so swiftly, they thought, that a collapse would take its trading partners completely by surprise. Instead, the U.S. central bank decided to provide Bear Stearns with emergency funding. Because Bear Stearns was a securities firm rather than a bank, though, the Fed had no jurisdiction over the company. It invoked an obscure rule, one which hadn't been used since the 1960s, to channel funds to Bear Stearns via JPMorgan, which was under the Fed's direct supervision.

On March 14, the Fed agreed to provide as much as a month's financing to Bear Stearns. In a statement after the Fed's announcement, the Securities and Exchange Commission (SEC) reiterated its view that Bear Stearns had "a substantial capital cushion" on March 11, based on the information that the company had supplied. "Beginning on that day, however, and increasingly throughout the week, lenders and customers of Bear Stearns began to remove funds from the firm," the SEC said. "As a result, Bear Stearns' excess liquidity rapidly eroded." Once the market lost faith in Bear, its days were numbered.

Rather than take comfort from the Fed's transfusion, the market smelled blood. Standard & Poor's slashed the securities firm's long-term counterparty rating by three levels, to BBB. Moody's cut the rating two steps to Baa1 and Fitch Ratings reduced the firm's grade by four levels. All three firms said they were considering whether further cuts were justified.

Market participants speculated that Bear Stearns would have to sell itself to JPMorgan; on March 16, JPMorgan agreed to buy Bear

Stearns for about $270 million, a discount of more than 90 percent to its market value less than a week earlier. The Fed propped up Bear Stearns for just two days.

To facilitate the nuptials, the Fed said it would provide a dowry, in the form of a $30 billion loan to JPMorgan, at 2.5 percent over a ten-year term. JPMorgan would use the money to take over Bear Stearns' assets, shouldering the first $1 billion of any losses. The government's money would backstop any further losses.

U.S. Treasury Secretary Henry Paulson said Bear Stearns' share price slump demonstrated that financial firms weren't enjoying preferential treatment, despite the government's role in arranging JP-Morgan's purchase, nor did the rescue package suggest that the authorities would sanction future risky behavior. "When we talk about moral hazard, I would say look at the Bear Stearns shareholder—this is what happens when there is a liquidity problem," Paulson said. After a shareholder rebellion against the cut-price offer, JPMorgan ultimately paid about $10 per share for Bear, higher than its initial $2 bid.

The Fed's initial rescue stratagem was formulated in haste, as a weekend approached. Participants knew Bear would struggle to survive when financial markets reopened on Monday morning. That may have made the situation worse. By focusing its support directly on Bear Stearns, the Fed turned the firm into a pariah, lessening its chances of surviving as an independent firm.

In April 2008, CEO Schwatz told the U.S. Congress that the Fed's actions singled out his firm. Had the central bank made funding more widely available to financial firms earlier in the year, that stigma might have been averted. "I do believe that as a policy measure, had the discount window been opened to investment banks for their high-quality collateral, I think it is highly, highly unlikely in my personal opinion that we would be in the situation we find ourselves in today," Schwartz told members of the Senate Banking Committee.

Schwartz was suggesting that Bear Stearns could have posted its bonds as collateral for a cash loan from the Fed, papering over the cracks that formed in its balance sheet as customers withdrew their funds. The Fed's rules, though, didn't allow a securities firm to borrow that way—though it changed those rules on March 16, the day Bear fell into JPMorgan's arms.

Belatedly, the Fed threw open the discount window to twenty primary dealers: firms that facilitate trading in U.S. government bonds by buying Treasury debt directly from the central bank. The rule change that Schwartz says might have saved Bear's independence came too late. The Fed also lowered the discount rate by a quarter of a percentage point, to 3.25 percent. It was the Fed's first weekend emergency action in almost three decades, and it signaled just how severe the crisis had become.

During the autopsy that followed Bear Stearns' demise, Fed chairman Ben Bernanke said regulators had no "early warning" to prepare for its collapse, as confidence and cash had drained away from the firm so quickly. He revealed that the firm's executives had warned the authorities on March 13 that, without new sources of funding, they might seek Chapter 11 bankruptcy protection, which would have sent terror rippling through the banking industry and economy.

"The adverse effects would not have been confined to the financial system but would have been felt broadly in the real economy through its effects on asset values and credit availability," Bernanke told the Joint Economic Committee of Congress at an April 2 hearing. "With financial conditions fragile, the sudden failure of Bear Stearns likely would have led to a chaotic unwinding of positions in those markets and could have severely shaken confidence."

Bernanke also suggested that the Fed-assisted rescue would not set a precedent. "The financing we did for Bear Stearns is a one-time event," he said. "It's never happened before and I hope it never happens again."

But Wall Street ignored his statement. Fannie Mae and Freddie Mac's implicit government guarantees had solidified into concrete financial backing; now the Fed had thrown Bear Stearns a lifeline. The Fed had blinked, and there was no reason to assume it wouldn't do so again, providing more lifeboats to sinking companies.

Even billionaire investor George Soros, revered as one of the world's savviest investors, was convinced that the Fed's actions would prevent the collapse of any more investment banks. "This phase of the crisis is over," Soros said in an April 2 television interview broadcast by CNBC. "The Fed is in the business of providing liquidity. It has gone so far in providing liquidity that it has taken considerable risk in taking on papers, mortgages, whose value is rather unknown."

Lehman Falls

Bear Stearns had looked like the weakest horse in the financial glue factory, but Lehman Brothers wasn't in much better shape. Indeed, its risk profile was very similar to that of Bear Stearns. Lehman, though, had one big advantage over the five biggest U.S. brokerage firms that were its peers. A decade earlier, it survived a liquidity crisis of its own, one that began with a collapse in confidence.

In July 1998, persistent gossip suggested Lehman was running out of cash and on the brink of insolvency. Speculative talk focused on the possibility of big losses in the bond market, which was Lehman's specialty and its main source of income at the time. CEO Richard Fuld decided to let the scaremongering burn itself out, a decision he came to regret. The firm lost more than half of its market value in four months, forcing him to belatedly embark on a successful charm offensive, reassuring clients of his firm's health.

After that save, Fuld broadened Lehman's horizons, attempting to reduce its future vulnerability. The firm moved away from the fixed income market, expanding its equity business until it was the fourth biggest stock trader on both the New York Stock Exchange and Nasdaq, up from its former position as sixth biggest. Fuld also expanded Lehman's corporate banking activities, making it the leading adviser on U.S. mergers and acquisitions by March 2008. A year earlier, the firm was in sixth place here, too.

Now Lehman was facing a new round of gossip, again speculating that it was in financial trouble. With the Fed escorting Bear Stearns down the aisle to its shotgun wedding to JPMorgan, Lehman's executives knew that dignified silence wouldn't protect it. On March 17, the day after Bear announced its betrothal, Lehman's shares dropped almost 40 percent, matching the first quarter's entire decline in just the first few hours of the day's trading session. Lehman issued a statement. "Our liquidity position has been and continues to be very strong," the firm said. What's more, Lehman's Fuld said, the Fed's decision to start lending money to the biggest government bond dealers "takes the liquidity issue for the entire industry off the table."

That was wishful thinking. On September 10, Lehman announced a $3.9 billion loss, the biggest in its history, after taking $5.6 billion of write-downs on directly held real-estate loans and mortgage-backed debt. By then, Lehman shares had dropped more than 90 percent for the year, and the company was worth less than $3 billion. A foreign investor, Korea Development Bank, offered to pay $6.40 a share, or a total of a bit more than $5 billion, for a controlling stake in Lehman, says Min Euoo Sung, the Korean bank's CEO. Lehman, though, wanted $17.50 per share. "There was a significant gap in the estimated price, which wasn't easy to close," so the talks collapsed, Min said.

By the second week in September, it was clear that Lehman couldn't survive alone. Court statements filed later that month show that Lehman bled more than $400 billion in just a couple of months, as customers lost faith in the firm.

The Federal Reserve Bank of New York looked for a company willing to purchase Lehman. On September 12, a Friday, a group including New York Fed chief Tim Geithner, Treasury secretary Henry Paulson, SEC chairman Christopher Cox, and the heads of as many as fourteen financial institutions gathered to discuss a salvage plan, according to Thomas Baxter, who attended the talks as general counsel to the New York Fed. With Bank of America busy making overtures to Merrill Lynch, the United Kingdom's Barclays Bank was Lehman's only potential suitor. But U.S. authorities weren't willing to guarantee Lehman's trading obligations during the period between a merger's announcement and its closing. The potential deal fell apart, leaving bankruptcy as the only viable outcome, Baxter told a London School of Economics conference in January 2009.

Merrill Sells

Lehman wasn't the only firm in trouble. Merrill Lynch was also struggling to survive, and had battled for months to shore up its defenses. In December 2007 it accepted a $4.4 billion investment from Temasek Holdings, a sovereign wealth fund controlled by Singapore's government, and began selling off assets and trying to clean up its balance sheet. In mid-July 2008, after reporting a $4.65 billion second-quarter net loss, CEO John Thain told his investors that that Merrill was "in a very comfortable spot in terms of our capital."

By the end of July, Thain announced that Merrill wasn't quite comfortable enough. The company, he said, wanted to raise an additional $8.55 billion of capital and was holding a clearance sale from its derivatives stockpile. Merrill took a third-quarter pretax write-down of $4.4 billion, in addition to the second-quarter $3.5 billion CDO write-down. Moreover, Merrill agreed to sell almost $31 billion of CDOs to an affiliate of Dallas-based investment manager Lone Star

Funds in a transaction that valued the securities at just 22 percent of their face value. To get the deal done, Merrill agreed to lend Lone Star three-quarters of the money it needed to fund the purchase. The loan relied on those same CDOs as collateral and was therefore exposed to any further deterioration in their value.

Such desperate measures bought time, though not salvation. On September 14, as Wall Street prepared Lehman's last rites, Merrill Lynch agreed to be taken over by Bank of America. Merrill's shareholders received $29 per share, a 70 percent premium to the stock's closing price the previous Friday, though that in turn was a 70 percent discount to the stock's high, which it reached in January 2007. Thain's willingness to face reality, swallow his pride, and sell the company to a rival delivered the best possible outcome for Merrill shareholders under the circumstances. Lehman might have followed Merrill's example, controlling its own destiny by finding a buyer at whatever price it could get.

It wasn't to be. As the Lehman talks continued, it became clear that the company was doomed. Treasury officials discreetly briefed journalists, telling them that Treasury secretary Henry Paulson wouldn't replicate Bear Stearns' rescue by using government money to salvage Lehman. Instead, the Fed's emergency lending program—which wasn't in place when Bear Stearns had difficulties—would help Lehman die in a quiet, orderly fashion, should the need arise. Besides, the briefings suggested, Wall Street had known for several months that another broker could go down, and had enjoyed more than enough time to brace for the consequences of a second failure.

The Safety Net That Wasn't

Those arguments were disingenuous at best. By pledging government money to facilitate the Bear Stearns purchase, the Fed inadvertently created false expectations. In the time since Bear Stearns' rescue, Wall Street had less incentive, not more, to adopt a defensive posture because traders thought that the Bear Stearns episode was definitive proof that the Fed would avert any other potential disasters by serving as the lender of last resort.

On September 15, unable to find a buyer and abandoned by both the government and central bank, Lehman folded—the biggest bankruptcy the world had ever seen. Lehman was 158 years old at its death. It had about 25,000 employees and owed more than $600 billion. Its ten largest unsecured creditors had claims worth more than $157 billion. The credit crunch had reached its climax.

The failure's repercussions immediately began to resonate. The Reserve Primary Fund, the oldest money market fund in the United States had lent Lehman $785 million of the $64.8 billion the Reserve Primary Fund managed for its customers. Those clients pulled out more than 60 percent of their money in the two days following Lehman's demise, and Reserve Primary, which had been in business since 1970, became the second money market fund ever to break the buck, with its assets worth a humiliating 97 cents for every dollar entrusted to it.

Lehman held billions of dollars in customer assets. All were immediately frozen, pending an investigation into what belonged to Lehman and what should be returned to clients, according to PricewaterhouseCoopers, the administrator handling the bankruptcy. Determining asset ownership was "exceptionally complex," Steven Pearson, a partner at PWC, said in a September 17 presentation. "We won't be in a position to transfer certain client accounts in the relatively short term. I can't give any clarity on when those assets will be transferred."

Other financial firms swiftly dismembered Lehman's corpse. Barclays, which had declined to attempt a full takeover, picked over the carcass, spending a bit more than $1.5 billion to acquire Lehman's North American investment banking and capital markets operations.

Nomura Holdings, Japan's biggest investment bank, paid $225 million for Lehman's Asian business, and what it described as a "nominal" sum for its European investment banking and equities businesses. Bain Capital and Hellman & Friedman spent a total $2.15 billion to buy Lehman's investment management unit, including its Neuberger Berman money manager division, which oversaw about $130 billion. That price also included part of a private equity group that invests in leveraged buyouts and real estate.

"We are now seeing what we regard as an unintended consequence of Paulson's decision not to give government support," Nigel Myer, a credit strategist at Dresdner Kleinwort in London, wrote in a September 26 research report. "It is a sensible strategy not to rescue a whole bank on an ongoing basis, but rather to wait for failure and then buy the bits you want at a knock-down price. Rescuers are waiting until after a failure before stepping in. This allows them to buy only certain assets and means they don't have to acquire all liabilities."

For AIG, Yet Another Policy Shift

It seemed that the new policy was to let nature take its course. The Fed, however, abandoned this new outlook within days, when the U.S. government took control of American International Group (AIG), averting a financial collapse that would have made Lehman's fall look puny.

In 2007, AIG revealed that it had $64 billion at risk in contracts representing AAA-rated CDO portions, known as "super senior" debt. That debt wasn't quite so super, after all; in the fourth quarter of that year, the eighty-nine-year-old insurer posted the biggest quarterly loss in its history. An $11 billion write-down in the value of its derivatives holdings caused the company to lose almost $5.3 billion in the final three months of 2007. The damage got worse. The insurance company posted consecutive losses of $18.5 billion over the course of the three quarters ending in the middle of 2008, after its Financial Products trading division generated about $25 billion in write-downs.

As a result, AIG needed a huge capital infusion—far more capital than the markets could supply. AIG had approached billionaire Warren Buffett in its efforts to raise enough additional capital to stay alive. "They needed more than we could supply by far," Buffett told Bloomberg Television in March 2009. "I didn't know the extent of it, but I knew that."

The Fed didn't have the power to unwind AIG, but it could and did take over the company. In exchange for a two-year loan worth an astonishing $85 billion, the Fed invoked emergency powers, took control of 79.9 percent of AIG's stock, and began replacing AIG's management. "A disorderly failure of AIG could add to already significant levels of financial market fragility," the Fed stated at the time.

AIG Financial Products had opened for business in 1987. Joseph Cassano, one of the unit's founders, ran it from London. AIG had been regulated by a government entity called the Office of Thrift Supervision since 2000, when it applied to form a federal savings bank. As a result, the financial products group flew under the radar, even as it built a $2.7 trillion derivatives business.

Because AIG's insurance business merited a top AAA credit rating, the company's derivatives operation enjoyed the same grade, letting it offer terms on deals that less creditworthy competitors couldn't match. "AIG exploited a huge gap in the regulatory system," explained Fed chairman Ben Bernanke. "There was no oversight of the financial products division. This was a hedge fund, basically, that was attached to a large and stable insurance company."

Even with the CDO market in meltdown, and with AIG's financial products group facing the prospect of paying out on billions of dollars in credit swaps, Cassano said in August 2007 that he couldn't imagine a situation in which AIG would lose "one dollar in any of these transactions." In the parlance of Wall Street, AIG was said to be "money good" in the long run, no matter how damaged it looked in the short term—and no matter how much money it lost. AIG posted net losses of almost $100 billion in 2008, the bulk of which came from its financial products division.

"The extent and interconnectedness of AIG's business is far-reaching and encompasses customers across the globe ranging from governmental agencies, corporations and consumers to counterparties," AIG itself said in a report it compiled in February 2009, pressuring the government into handing over more cash. "A failure of AIG could create a chain reaction of enormous proportion."

That, at least, was true: an AIG bankruptcy would have been hazardous, as even a single example shows. AIG's International Lease Finance Corporation unit owned the most valuable fleet of airplanes in the world, with more than 950 aircraft leased to a variety of commercial customers. In the aftermath of an AIG bankruptcy, administrators might ground those planes as AIG assets. Overnight, the world's airlines and freight companies would discover that those leased planes would not be available when needed.

Companies associated with AIG suffered from the connection. Songbird Estates, which was Lehman's London landlord, saw its shares drop 15 percent after the Fed took over its tenant. Songbird had insurance to cover Lehman's rent on the offices it occupied in the Canary Wharf district—but its protection came from AIG. The U.S. government's rescue of AIG let Songbird successfully make a claim on its policy.

The fallout continued to spread. S&P rated 1,889 CDOs whose values were tied in part to the Lehman's creditworthiness. The rating company also assessed 1,619 transactions linked to AIG. These deals weren't isolated; many linked simultaneously to both firms, and so already battered CDOs took more rating downgrades and corresponding drops in value.

By March 2009, the U.S. government had pumped about $170 billion into AIG. Some $52 billion of that went to AIG's customers who were owed money on credit-default swap contracts AIG had sold them, including almost $13 billion to Goldman Sachs, $12 billion to France's Société Générale $12 billion to Germany's Deutsche Bank, and more than $8 billion to the United Kingdom Barclays Bank. The payouts were substantially more than creditors might have recovered in an AIG bankruptcy. American taxpayers were footing the bill for AIG's wanton profligacy.

Taxpayers weren't happy about that handout, and became even angrier when news broke that AIG paid staff $165 million in guaranteed bonuses, also in March 2009. The payments triggered a bitter debate about the ethics of rewarding failure. Those bonuses were outrageous. Reneging on the contracts, however, safe in the knowledge that the public was in the mood for a lynching, would have been even more scandalous.

Public anger at the financial industry's failures became widespread; some firms even used that rage as a handy marketing tool. In September 2008, Krispy Kreme Doughnuts had offered "kredit krunch treats," or twelve deep-fried treats for the price of seven. By March 2009, Domino's Pizza ran U.S. television advertisements heralding a $5 pizza deal for regular workers; the spot condemned the "fat cats on Wall Street" as unworthy of such generosity.

Credit Crunch Climax

Lehman's collapse and AIG's rescue brought a renewed wave of speculation about other potential bankruptcies among financial companies. It was an ideal situation for short sellers—investors who try to profit from declining stocks by selling shares they don't own in the hope of buying at future, lower prices—but regulators moved to block any attempt to profit from sliding stock prices. On September 18 the United Kingdom Financial Services Authority slapped a four-month ban on short sales of British financial companies' stock. The Securities and Exchange Commission (SEC) quickly imposed a similar prohibition in the United States and began investigating whether some hedge funds were spreading malicious gossip to drive down financial firms' share prices.

The actions showed that the authorities were still at least partly in the dark about the credit crunch's true causes. Financial firms' stock prices were crumbling because their assets were rotten to the core and they didn't have sufficient capital, not because an evil whispering campaign spread unfounded rumors. An entire branch of the hedge fund industry was dedicated to making money from betting which share prices were overvalued and headed for a drop—an entirely legitimate investment strategy, and one that had also profited the proprietary trading desks at investment banks for years. The short-selling ban was nothing more than a misguided search for scapegoats. The true villains were clearly the bankers themselves, not the stock market speculators.

The U.S. authorities underwent a change of heart in the months following their decision to underwrite JPMorgan's takeover of Bear Stearns. In the heat of the moment, allowing a major securities firm such as Bear to go under had seemed untenable. Lehman, though, had been a much slower-moving train wreck, giving officials sufficient space to become comfortable with staying on the sidelines. Letting Lehman go bust felt like the right thing to do; it would cleanse moral hazard from the system and show the market that regulators were ready to let natural selection operate in the business world. Lehman's death would prove, once and for all, that the Bear Stearns bailout truly was a one-time exercise.

That, at least, was the theory. In practice, the authorities appeared schizophrenic. The Fed tossed a $29 billion parachute to Bear Stearns as it plummeted to the ground; investors had assumed similar safety devices would be freely available to other credit crunch victims. Instead, they discovered that regulators would now allow gravity to run its course. Lehman's fall meant that the entire U.S. banking system lost its perceived, Fed-issued safety net, leaving the finance industry in limbo.

With hindsight, the U.S. government should either have rescued both Bear Stearns and Lehman Brothers, or neither of them. Letting Bear go bankrupt would probably have forced Lehman to find a way to sell itself before it was too late, just as Merrill Lynch did. Moreover, had the authorities realized how close AIG was to following Lehman off bankruptcy's cliff, they would probably have offered the parachute option for a second time. The inconsistency of the response destroyed any remaining vestiges of trust in the financial system.

As European Central Bank member Miguel Ángel Fernández Ordóñez put it about a month after the credit crunch climax, the decision to allow Lehman to disintegrate led to an "absolute loss of confidence in markets." That confidence will take years to recover—if it ever does.

ELEVEN

Conclusions and Policy Prescriptions

PSYCHIATRY SUGGESTS that people whose lives have been engulfed by catastrophe follow a predictable coping pattern. They start off engulfed in denial, try to bargain their way out of the dilemma, then succumb to depression before finally accepting their misfortune and resuming their lives as best they can. Unfortunately, most of the financial industry hasn't even made it to the first stage. Too many bankers are acting as if the disaster never happened.

The financial industry's siren song is easy to summarize. Regulate us too strictly, the bankers say, and global growth will suffer. Never mind that this argument assumes that banks cannot innovate and that self-regulating is precisely what brought the economy crashing down. The banking community hasn't made amends for its profligate behavior. Indeed, it will always find ways to argue that business as usual is the only way to safeguard the global economy.

Government-sponsored mergers and opportunistic purchases will mean fewer and larger banks in the landscape that emerges after the credit crunch's dust settles. Governments, however, cannot allow these banks to dictate policy and must ignore finance chiefs

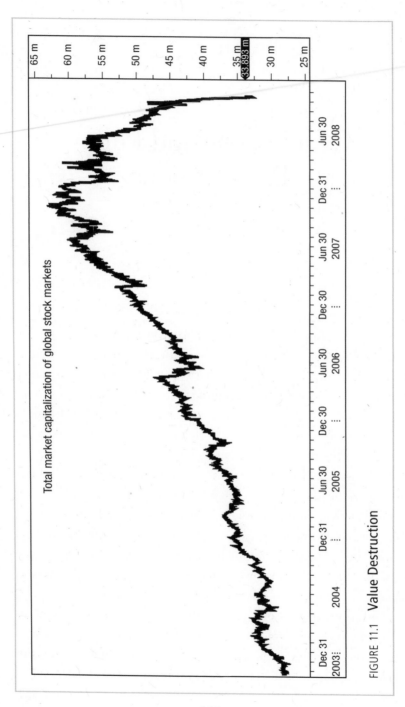

FIGURE 11.1 Value Destruction

who bleat at the prospect of new rules. The market needs safety strictures, even if new safeguards make it harder for investment banking to invent and profit from new techniques and strategies. Following is a list of changes designed to protect us from the worst excesses of the finance industry, without killing its ability to contribute to the global economy.

Moral Hazard

In this credit crunch, national regulators rescued at least some failing institutions. In doing so, they have essentially committed to future rescues. "The government has dispelled any constructive ambiguity on how far it's willing to let banks and investors suffer," former Bank of England Deputy Governor John Gieve said in June 2009. "There's now a safety net covering every significant bank, even banks that have failed. Moral hazard is a real issue now."

Moreover, it turns out that the riskier an institution is, the higher its chances of a government rescue. If regulators had seen Lehman as posing a threat equal to that of Bear Stearns, a government-guaranteed transaction might have saved Lehman, too. Bankers now have concrete evidence that maximizing the economic dangers posed by their businesses is the best way to ensure their survival.

To avoid this moral hazard, nations must force banks to set aside sufficient capital to cover unexpected disasters. Regulators should compel the banking industry to insure itself, with each institution making regular payments into an insurance pool. Institutions that aren't fit should be allowed to die. "Banks have to be free to make decisions and therefore to fail," says Bill Blain, a bond broker at KNG Securities in London. "That is the unfortunate issue to address: how to allow the banking industry the efficiency to fail."

The supervision system in place for the past decade paid almost no attention to the financial world's interconnections. A new approach must take a broader view, testing the overall system rather than just its constituent parts. As Fed chairman Ben Bernanke said in July 2009, regulators have to take into account "the safety and soundness of the financial system as a whole, as well as individual institutions."

New rules must also recognize that size matters. "Banks must resume lending, but they must also adjust by becoming smaller, simpler, and safer," the Bank for International Settlements said in its June 2009 annual report. "Government rescue packages implemented so far appear to be hindering rather than aiding this needed adjustment. By helping banks obtain debt financing and capital, rescue packages allow managers to avoid the hard choices needed." Moreover, the BIS said, shotgun weddings among failing institutions create "financial institutions so big and complex that even their own management may not understand their risk exposures."

As financial institutions don't seem to have natural size limits—the cumulative assets of UBS and Credit Suisse, the two biggest banks in Switzerland, grew to six times the size of the entire Swiss economy during the credit boom—regulators will have to impose artificial size restrictions. "We attach particular importance to alleviating the 'too big to fail' problem," Swiss central bank chairman Philipp Hildebrand said in June 2009. "There can be no more taboos, given our experiences of the last two years." Governments should give themselves the power to intervene to stop banks from becoming too large, abandoning the hands-off approach and admitting that finance is just too dangerous and too important to be allowed to grow unfettered.

Don't Bank on Academia

Central banking is far too important to be run by academics, a circumstance that currently prevails in much of the world. These unelected apparatchiks have worldviews shaped by textbooks and conferences—not the demands of the business world.

Every rate-setting committee at every central bank in every country should be obliged to reserve several places at the table for business-people, preferably those who have built companies from scratch and have the welfare of several hundred workers weighing on their minds.

Entrepreneurs know how to run a business, understand the practical implications of the decisions central banks make, and are intimately in tune with the real economy. That makes them ideal guardians of monetary stability. There's a risk that they might consistently favor lower borrowing costs than their more scholastic colleagues. That need not be a bad thing, given the anti-inflationary zealotry that is currently in fashion. It seems plausible to suggest that a better mix of backgrounds and experience would lead to better policymaking.

A true capitalist model, on the other hand, might completely dispense with the human touch. We might allow the free market to dictate the price of money everywhere and anywhere, instead of reserving special market corners for central bank oversight. (Given the prevailing lack of trust in market rationality, however, that might prove even less popular than the current system.)

Ratings for Sale

The current business model lets financial product creators pay for the ratings they need to sell those products to investors, a system that has proven itself utterly corrupt. Investors have lost all trust in the grading system. Collusion between assayers and sellers was directly responsible for the boom in complicated investment instruments, many of which should never have been stamped with top credit grades.

It's probably too late to legislate the rating companies out of existence. Removing them in one fell swoop could shock the markets into paralysis. Displacing ratings from their central role in determining asset risk will take years of tweaking the rules that govern accounting and capital adequacy. Creating a government ratings agency isn't an option either because no investor would accept a civil servant's verdict on an investment's credit quality.

Instead, market forces should produce a Darwinist solution. Those who use ratings—not those who commission them—should pay for their production. Ratings companies will either learn to live with the new framework or, if investors don't value their work enough to pay for it, they will (and should) wither and die. Finance abhors a vacuum at least as much as the rest of the universe, and it will find another way to meet investor needs if current ratings companies fall.

To facilitate that change, governments should stop letting ratings companies use nonpublic information to make their judgments. Everyone should have access to the same data, removing Moody's and S&P's current advantage. Investors could rely on their own judgments without the risk that concealed unknowns might make a homegrown analysis worthless. Alternatively, a thousand ratings companies might bloom, and the fittest would survive and prosper while the inadequate perish.

Payment in Kind

A bonus system that lets the banking community profit (but never suffer) from reckless gambling is untenable. The days of playing now but discovering the consequences later must end. Bankers once argued that they were locked into their institutions' equity performance; this has proven false.

The authorities have a right to play a part in redrafting the financial world's compensation system, though only because taxpayers have footed the bill for finance's disastrous exploits. Even now, though, numerical caps make no sense, no matter how well they play to the gallery. The government should not determine how much money a smart, talented individual can earn in finance, sports, acting, or any other field, no matter how obscene the payouts might appear to regular folk.

A possible solution might give greater weight to the amount of risk a bank takes to achieve its profits, with more speculative adventures generating lower bonuses. That would help reduce traders' temptation to bet the ranch. Techniques that measure risk in proportion to reward are far from perfect, but using them would still be better than not attempting the exercise at all.

Paying bankers in kind could be the best way of aligning risk-takers' interests with those of the stakeholders they serve. Had American International Group paid its management and traders in super-senior credit-default swaps, its executives might have spent more time analyzing whether those securities were as super as they first seemed.

Companies should also employ mechanisms to claw back bonuses that are based on chimerical returns. Traders shouldn't be able to skip town with bags full of cash, leaving their former employers owning investments that sour over several years.

Switzerland's Credit Suisse has made some voluntary changes to the ways in which it compensates its employees; these seem to be on the right track. Bank rules allow it to recoup payments in subsequent years if trades later go awry; the bank is also using securities, including mortgage-backed bonds and leveraged loans, to pay its senior staff, exposing them to the same risks that Credit Suisse shareholders face. In the boom times, chief executives didn't want the prospect of repaying their own bonuses, and so didn't inflict a similar constraint on their traders. If banks prove unwilling to alter their payment structures, governments should do it for them.

Don't Take My Money to the Casino

Legislators enacted the Glass-Steagall laws in 1933 to separate commercial banking from investment banking. They thought the Great

Depression had revealed the dangers of commingling the two. U.S. President Bill Clinton's administration dismantled those laws in 1999, a change that likely helped cause the credit crisis. The old rules, it seemed, were better at protecting ordinary bank customers than banking lobbyists—who clamored for the rule change—would ever admit. "We are going to have to grasp the issue of actually splitting off the casinos from the traditional kind of utility banking," Vince Cable, a U.K. politician who speaks on economic policy for the opposition Liberal Democrats, said in June 2009.

An American regulator agreed. Former Federal Reserve chairman Paul Volcker, now head of President Barack Obama's Economic Recovery Advisory Board, said in April that while he wouldn't want to bring the act back in full, dividing commercial banking from the more risk-seeking ventures is desirable.

"I want to separate the service-oriented core of the system from capital market trading, which is of course very risky," he said. "A lot of money is in markets, particularly in so-called proprietary trading, where people are out there trading things they have no intrinsic interest in. They're trading to make money. And that I would leave away from the banks."

It is difficult to decide which areas of banking should or shouldn't rub shoulders with ordinary savings and checking accounts, but that's no excuse for not making the effort. Maybe, though, the government is the only institution that can really be trusted to look after deposits. It's their only protector, it seems, in the event of a systemic disaster.

Bursting Bubbles

The events of recent years suggest that ignoring the housing market—or any other credit bubble—is folly.

"The spectacle of banking runs, asset price reversals, and economic imbalances testifies that the inflation targeting framework as currently operated is not sufficient," Bank of England chief economist Spencer Dale told a conference organized by Norway's central bank in Oslo in June 2009. "Recent events must serve as a wakeup call for policy makers. The ideal would be policy instruments that are effective in insuring against the build-up of asset price bubbles and imbalances."

Central bankers must overcome their philosophical objections to popping bubbles before they grow big enough to pose an economic threat. Monetary policy must never again be left on hold while an asset bubble swells to the bursting point. Moreover, bank capital adequacy rules must be flexible. At the first sign that the financial community is off to the races again, regulators should tighten the reins.

Test for Testosterone

In July 2009, a committee set up by the U.K. Treasury opened an inquiry into the role of "Women in the City" as part of its broader investigation into the banking crisis. The panel said it would examine pay equality, glass ceilings, sexism, and what proportion of senior positions women occupy in the major U.K. financial institutions.

The answer to that final question is easy. Globally, banking management is still very much a male-dominated milieu. It would be an exaggeration to say that not a single woman played a part in the credit crunch, of course, but it would be hard to overemphasize the role played by the macho culture in which the seeds of the banking crisis germinated. A government-mandated quota system, one that would move more women into senior management and onto executive boards, would be tricky to implement and difficult to enforce. It still might be worth trying.

Index

About the Author

Mark Gilbert is London bureau chief and a columnist on global capital markets for Bloomberg News, and has been with the company since 1991. Gilbert was born in Liverpool and graduated from Kings College, Cambridge, in 1989 with a BA (Hons) in philosophy. He was nominated as a finalist in the commentary category of the U.K. 2006 Business Journalist of the Year awards, and holds a Malcolm Forbes Award for Best Business Story from the Overseas Press Club of America. He plays bass guitar in a rock band.

About Bloomberg

Bloomberg L.P., founded in 1981, is a global information services, news, and media company. Headquartered in New York, the company has sales and news operations worldwide.

Serving customers on six continents, Bloomberg, through its wholly-owned subsidiary Bloomberg Finance L.P., holds a unique position within the financial services industry by providing an unparalleled range of features in a single package known as the Bloomberg Professional® service. By addressing the demand for investment performance and efficiency through an exceptional combination of information, analytic, electronic trading, and straight-through-processing tools, Bloomberg has built a worldwide customer base of corporations, issuers, financial intermediaries, and institutional investors.

Bloomberg News, founded in 1990, provides stories and columns on business, general news, politics, and sports to leading newspapers and magazines throughout the world. Bloomberg Television, a 24-hour business and financial news network, is produced and distributed globally in seven languages. Bloomberg Radio is an international radio network anchored by flagship station Bloomberg 1130 (WBBR-AM) in New York.

In addition to the Bloomberg Press line of books, Bloomberg publishes *Bloomberg Markets* magazine. To learn more about Bloomberg, call a sales representative at:

London:	+44-20-7330-7500
New York:	+1-212-318-2000
Tokyo:	+81-3-3201-8900